THE ETHICS
OF BUSINESS

ELEMENTS OF PHILOSOPHY

The Elements of Philosophy series aims to produce core introductory texts in the major areas of philosophy, among them metaphysics, epistemology, ethics and moral theory, philosophy of religion, philosophy of mind, aesthetics and the philosophy of art, feminist philosophy, and social and political philosophy. Books in the series are written for an undergraduate audience of second- through fourth-year students and serve as the perfect cornerstone for understanding the various elements of philosophy.

Moral Theory: An Introduction by Mark Timmons

An Introduction to Social and Political Philosophy: A Question-Based Approach by Richard Schmitt

Epistemology: Classic Problems and Contemporary Responses, Second Edition, by Laurence BonJour

Aesthetics and the Philosophy of Art: An Introduction, Second Edition, by Robert Stecker

Aesthetics Today: A Reader edited by Robert Stecker and Ted Gracyk

Introduction to Ethics: A Reader edited by Andrew J. Dell'Olio and Caroline J. Simon

The Ethics of Business: A Concise Introduction by Al Gini and Alexei Marcoux

THE ETHICS OF BUSINESS

A CONCISE INTRODUCTION

Al Gini and Alexei Marcoux

ROWMAN & LITTLEFIELD PUBLISHERS, INC.
Lanham • Boulder • New York • Toronto • Plymouth, UK

Published by Rowman & Littlefield Publishers, Inc.
A wholly owned subsidiary of The Rowman & Littlefield Publishing Group, Inc.
4501 Forbes Boulevard, Suite 200, Lanham, Maryland 20706
http://www.rowmanlittlefield.com

Estover Road, Plymouth PL6 7PY, United Kingdom

British Library Cataloguing in Publication Information Available

Library of Congress Cataloging-in-Publication Data
Gini, Al, 1944-
  The ethics of business : a concise introduction / Al Gini and Alexei Marcoux.
      p. cm.
    Includes bibliographical references and index.
    ISBN 978-0-7425-6161-8 (cloth : alk. paper) -- ISBN 978-0-7425-6162-5
    (pbk. : alk. paper) -- ISBN 978-1-4422-1434-7 (ebook : alk. paper)
  1. Business ethics. I. Marcoux, Alexei M. II. Title.
  HF5387.G555 2010
  174'.4–dc23   2011030651

∞ ™ The paper used in this publication meets the minimum requirements
of American National Standard for Information Sciences—Permanence of
Paper for Printed Library Materials, ANSI/NISO Z39.48-1992.

Printed in the United States of America

1

THE PROJECT
AND THE PLAN

The purpose of life is . . . to be useful, to be honorable, to be compassionate, to have it makes some difference that you have lived and lived well.

—Ralph Waldo Emerson

BIG QUESTIONS

Some say philosophy can be reduced to three fundamental questions. We, as human beings, spend our lives either trying to evade them or struggling to resolve them. They are:

1. Where am I, and how came all of this to be?
2. What do I know, and how can I be sure of it?
3. What should I do?[1]

The first question is what philosophers call *metaphysics*—the study of the ultimate cause(s), purpose, and meaning of life and existence. Metaphysics seeks the ultimate *why* of the world. In Blaise Pascal's words, it asks, "Why am I here rather than there? Why am I now rather than then? Why am I at all?"

The second question is the domain of *epistemology*—the study of knowledge and how we can discover truth and falsity. Bertrand Russell cleverly phrased epistemology's central questions as, "How do we know? And how do we know we know it?"

Although both of these questions arise out of our natural curiosity about the world around us, their resolution exists outside the normal frame of things. The only way to address them is by means of conjecture, hypothesis, and theory. There doesn't seem to be an easy, practical, or hands-on way to confront and resolve them—if they are at all, in fact, resolvable.

These kinds of questions are daunting, intimidating, and disheartening. Their size and reach tend to blunt our interest and willingness to pursue them. Even those professional philosophers who do pursue them too often end up with analyses and answers that only make sense to other similarly trained thinkers. As a psychologist and pundit, Robert R. Provine has suggested the pursuit of philosophy may stir up the imagination, create curious and interesting questions, and fire up the passions, but in the end the answers too often fall short. He believes that philosophers fail because they have "an overly optimistic estimate of the power of naked reason and a dependence on anecdotal evidence."[2]

ETHICS

Of the three central questions of philosophy, perhaps the only one we cannot in some way avoid is the last one, "What should I do?" This question is the domain of *ethics*. It presses on us in a way the others don't because we are "doomed," in Jean-Paul Sartre's words, to be free. We cannot escape choice and action except by escaping life itself. As if to illustrate the point, in their song "Freewill" the rock band Rush reminds us that "If you choose not to decide / You still have made a choice."

As a personal pursuit, we know historically that ethics has been around at least since the time of Socrates. As an academic discipline,

ethics has a long and rich history. There are many different schools of thought or theories regarding the ethical enterprise. These theories range from Aristotle's virtue ethics to Thomas Hobbes's concept of a social contract that governs our relations with one another; from Immanuel Kant's logic of duty to Jeremy Bentham's and John Stuart Mill's utilitarianism; from Thomas Aquinas's natural law theory to the philosophically inclined novelist Ayn Rand's objectivist ethics; from Jean-Paul Sartre's radical existentialism to David Gauthier's *Morals by Agreement*. Although these ethical theories, and a long list of others, offer radically different approaches and perspectives on what constitutes a morally acceptable act, they are all equally committed to answering the same philosophical question: How should we live? They also share a common set of presuppositions about the human condition:

1. Belief that life is important, valuable, or sacred.
2. Belief that no individual self is the center of the universe.
3. Belief that all individuals have and share certain basic rights.
4. Belief that all individuals have and share certain basic duties.[3]

INSPIRATION

In 1986, James Rachels published a little book on ethics that has become a classic in the field. *The Elements of Moral Philosophy* is an attempt to explain and unpack the major moral traditions in Western philosophy. As Rachels points out, the task is a daunting one and much too large to be covered in one book. So, decisions had to be made. What Rachels offers the reader is a superb synthesis of the general enterprise of ethics and a "minimal conception" of what morality is about. For Rachels, ethics is primarily a communal pursuit, not a solitary one. It is the study of our web of relations with others. Ethics is an attempt to work out rationally how we "ought to live with others." As creatures of reason, says Rachels, it is our duty to have good, rational arguments for our moral actions. For

Rachels, ethics is first and last an exercise in *reason*. Reasons count, and the best reasons win. In twelve succinct and well-written chapters, Rachels attempts to offer the general reader an overview of the major schools of ethical thought.

Rachels argues that philosophy is not like physics. In physics there is an established body of truths that, through rigorous and repeated application of the scientific method, are effectively beyond dispute and discussion. Philosophers, by contrast, debate and disagree even about the most fundamental of matters. Nevertheless, Rachels offers his "minimum conception of morality" as a means of addressing the Socratic challenge of "how we ought to live."

The minimum conception may be stated very briefly: Morality is, at the very least, the effort to guide one's conduct by reason—that is, to do what there are the best reasons for doing—while giving equal weight to the interests of each individual who will be affected by one's conduct.

This gives us, among other things, a picture of what it means to be a conscientious moral agent. The conscientious moral agent is someone who is concerned impartially with the interests of everyone affected by what he or she does; who carefully sifts facts only after scrutinizing them to make sure they are sound; who is willing to "listen to reason" even when it means that his or her earlier convictions may have to be revised; and who, finally, is willing to act on the results of this deliberation.[4]

The present book, *The Ethics in Business: A Concise Introduction*, is an attempt to apply Rachels's general methodology to the field of business ethics. In the last forty years, that field has matured into an important intellectual discipline for addressing the question of how we ought to work with and do business with others. Like ethics itself, this topic is too big to be covered in one volume. Consequently, we too want to offer something like a "minimal conception" of business ethics. Business ethics is a contextual part of ethics. It is best thought of as a way of life, a way of looking at the world, and a method of analysis.

BUSINESS ETHICS

In 1968, when Raymond C. Baumhart, S.J., published his ground-breaking text, *An Honest Profit: What Businessmen Say about Ethics in Business,* his intentions were quite modest. His attempt was to survey what *business persons* thought about, believed in, and actually did in regard to ethics in their business lives. By his own admission, Baumhart never consciously set out to create or anticipate the study of business ethics as a formal discipline. His book does not cover all of the major categories and issues in the field of business ethics, but in publishing it he, in fact, helped to initiate an important area of study as we know it today.

"Ours is a business-centered society," said Baumhart. "No group in America is more influential than *business persons*. Their influence, for good and evil, enters every life and every home . . . As Henry Ford II observed: 'Around the world we are often described as a business society.' If that is so, and if it is judged that *businesses* are corrupt, then it will be assumed that society itself is corrupt."[5] What is important to recognize is that Baumhart made the *person doing business* the object and focus of his study. He wanted to understand how and why individual business persons make the moral choices they do in the context of actually doing business. His inference, we think, is clear: Individuals, not institutions, are the loci of moral decision making and moral responsibility.

Since the publication of *An Honest Profit,* business ethics as a formal discipline has been a growth industry. Like most any academic discipline, over time it has become more focused and specialized in both its research and teaching. How can it be otherwise when you consider the complexity of the modern world of business: the global marketplace, international banking and finance, and our instantaneous online interconnectivity? However, it does not follow neatly from the fact that business is more complex that the *moral features* of business are more complex. As one NPR commentator has suggested, the sins and foibles we find in today's headlines ("Bernie Madoff Bilks Clients out of $65 Billion") are not different in kind

from the headlines of the past ("Charles Ponzi Dupes $20 Million from His Unsuspecting Customers"). In the end, the moral failures of business are the moral failures of business persons.

WHY THIS BOOK?

Business Ethics Books

There is no shortage of business ethics books. Textbooks, casebooks, and anthologies—they are numerous, and their numbers are growing. However, we believe that the prevailing approaches continue to leave an important space unfilled. The representative business ethics text focuses almost exclusively on the large corporation whose ownership shares are traded on public exchanges. Because so many of the issues taken up turn on the *scale* of the enterprise, the representative business ethics text is often more about bigness than about business. To the business ethics student, there is an implied "in case you ever become a C-level executive at a Fortune 500 company, you should (or shouldn't) do this" prefacing the discussion. The topics often have no or a very weak analogue to the circumstances of smaller-scale enterprises and entrepreneurial startups—the enterprises in which the overwhelming majority of business people work and do business. We believe that a book devoted to the *elements* of ethical business practice should be scalable. That is, it should speak to doing business in firms of whatever size; articulating an ethical landscape relevant to both the sole entrepreneur and the Fortune 500 CEO. It should say what is common to the ethics of business in *all* its forms, not what is peculiar to one of them.

The representative business ethics text has also a reformist orientation. Whether intended or not, it communicates the idea that business has an inherent moral deficiency and is thus in need of institutional reform and correction. In other words, business needs some ethics injected into it. While we certainly don't believe that business is perfect or beyond beneficial reform, we do believe that this approach sends the wrong message about business and about ethics. About business, it suggests that amoral or immoral activity is

the rule, rather than a deviation from the basic integrity that marks the bulk of business activity. Whether it be Enron's bookkeeping or Bernard Madoff's larceny, the capacity of business scandals to *shock* us illustrates that we both expect and experience honesty and transparency in the ordinary course of business. This belies the second impression that many business ethics texts leave; namely, that ethics is foreign to, and thus inherently reformative of, business. To the contrary, we believe that choosing to do business with another person entails a set of moral values, virtues, and commitments that together express a conception of *commercial integrity*. This conception allows even seasoned business people to be shocked by and condemn the Enrons and Madoffs of this world—and do so without first reading a business ethics text. Consequently, we believe that a worthwhile business ethics book should acknowledge and take some care in articulating this conception of commercial integrity.

We aim to negotiate a path between two deficient extremes. One extreme argues that there is no place for ethics in business. Ethics stops where business begins, and that's the way things ought to be. The other extreme sees business as morally irredeemable and ethics as a strategy for overcoming business practice. Though seemingly divergent, these views share a caricature and a common understanding of business and of ethics. Both hold that ethics undermines business. They disagree only about whether subverting business through ethics is desirable.

How This Book Is Different

Through a carefully developed account of what business is and what ethics is, we hope to show that business practice has an inherent ethical structure and entails a moral point of view. A better appreciation of its ethical structure offers a platform from which to see that the issue in business ethics is less "What's wrong with business?" than "Why is it hard to be good?"

Minimally, we want to argue that as rational creatures doing business with others, we are rightly concerned about their rights and well-being. What is more, this is implied in the very structure

of the most basic business acts: bargaining and exchange. Ethics in business, like ethics in everyday life, does not allow us to think of ourselves as the sole center of the universe. To do business with another—as opposed to raping, pillaging, or plundering him—requires regarding him both as a locus of moral value (a person deserving of respect) and as a responsible agent (an independent actor). This idea is pursued in more detail in chapter 4.

Like Rachels's effort, ours is an attempt to articulate the minimal content of business ethics. It will be minimal in two senses. First, it will describe the moral content of a specific human activity, business, rather than the moral contours of a fully just society. Second, this content will apply to business activity in any society having the basic institutions that support it. Like Rachels, our attempt is to reach out, to teach, to clarify, to make accessible and understandable what is usually taken to be a complicated topic.

To that end, the issues we address in this book are neither new nor esoteric. The Talmud is a 1,500-year-old text. It contains over two million words. A book of faith and commitment, it speaks of life lessons and the trials and sadness of life. Embedded throughout the text are approximately 613 commandments and directives regarding social and cultural customs and standards of behavior. There are also over a hundred rules directly speaking to and defining acceptable conduct in regard to business and economics.[6] These rules speak directly to the fact that human beings are liable to err and are easily deceived or mistaken, even when they have the best of intentions. Rules like these can often help; not always or even primarily by being punitive. They can also be prescriptive, allowing us to better establish our bearings and find our way. By the same token, the moral norms of business are not always or even primarily punitive. Like the Talmud or the law of contracts, business ethics is as much about showing us the right way to get what we want as about telling us what we cannot have.

A book on business ethics should be about business. Although it seems strange so say, it needs saying. For "business ethics" is often pursued as if it were more about evaluating economic institutions or criticizing features of organizational life than about the activities that

are basic to business. We believe that the elements of ethical business practice apply to business in any basically capitalist economy, whether that be the dynamic, free economy of Hong Kong or the stability-seeking "social market" economies of Western Europe. Wherever people have private property and are mainly free to relinquish and acquire it through bargaining and exchange, an elemental account of ethical business practice should be at home with doing business there. Thus, an *elemental* business ethics should have nothing to say about whether, all things considered, Anglo-American economic institutions are morally superior (or inferior) to Western European, social market ones. Both of those kinds of institutions recognize private property rights and mostly respect the right to relinquish and acquire private property through bargaining and exchange. That activity—the activity they share in common—defines business. Its moral contours are fundamental to an elemental business ethics.

A book about business ethics should be written first for business people, both actual and potential. It should not let academic enthusiasms trump its usefulness to its intended audience. As an example of what we mean, consider the following. An elementary school teacher of our acquaintance once said that teaching children about punctuation is a funny thing. After introducing them to the comma (,), on their next assignment her, students, almost, invariably, place, a, comma, after, every, word, they, write. In other words, they move immediately from complete ignorance of the comma to seeing every space between two words as an occasion for using it. There is something analogous at work in teaching applied ethics disciplines such as business ethics. Because ethical theories are theories about justification, the cases most interesting to rival theorists are cases in which the choice among alternatives depends on the justificatory framework you adopt. In other words, the most interesting cases are *dilemmas*. Although focusing on dilemmas is useful for deriving and criticizing ethical theories, it can have a misleading and counterproductive effect on applied ethics education. Just as the child introduced to the comma soon sees every word as an occasion to use it, the applied ethics student taught ethics through dilemmas is encouraged to see every moral choice situation as a dilemma.

By definition, a dilemma is a situation in which you are forced to choose between two or more equally compelling alternatives, each of which precludes (or negates) the other(s). If you are to choose between the alternatives in *theory*, you have to work out which justificatory framework (rational moral theory) is better than all the others—something that philosophers have been unable to do for the entire history of moral philosophy. If you are to choose between the alternatives in *practice*, it has to be on the basis of some *other* consideration—for example, prudence, self-interest, expediency, aesthetic beauty, etc. Consequently, to believe that moral choice situations are principally dilemmas invites the further belief that all choices are equally worthy (or unworthy) morally and one might as well choose on the basis of whatever other criteria one finds attractive or convenient. In other words, dilemmas invite the conclusion that anything goes. It suggests that we can't guide our actions by moral reasons—a conclusion we argue against in this book.

Our point in bringing this up is not to deny that dilemmas are real. Of course they are. It is instead to argue that, as important as it is to recognize dilemmas where they exist, it even is more important to recognize the more numerous cases where they don't exist. Because dilemmas are insoluble (otherwise they wouldn't be dilemmas), it is critical that we not encourage people to overidentify them. However, a focus on ethical theories and the dilemmas illustrating the differences between them invites exactly that. The morally earnest person under the delusion that dilemmas are everywhere despairs. The morally indifferent person under the same delusion marvels at the freedom of action dilemmas bring.

We believe that applied ethics is more profitably approached in a way that focuses on *action-guiding principles* rather than principles of justification; that is, principles that tell you *what* you ought to do rather than *why* you ought to do it. The point is not that justification is unimportant. However, it's more important to know what makes an easy case easy than to know what makes a hard case hard. Easy cases are easy because they are covered by an action-guiding principle justifiable from a variety of perspectives. Such a principle is uninteresting to the ethical theorist. To the participant in a practice

To Sherry L. Gini and Arianne Marcoux,
for their patience and support

CONTENTS

such as business, by contrast, that uninteresting principle is golden. It allows him to act with moral confidence. Consequently, an elemental business ethics should supply the business person with (in Ed Soule's words) "a few good principles"—principles of action that don't rest on the peculiar justification of a single, highly contestable moral theory.[7]

STRUCTURE AND USE

Structure

The representative business ethics text takes a *topical* approach, dividing its subject into what are sometimes called the "functional areas of business." In most every business ethics textbook you will find a chapter on marketing ethics, on management ethics, on accounting ethics, on finance ethics, and so forth. In addition, you may find chapters on international business, "corporate social responsibility," and (increasingly) the environment. It is as if the author organized the book by looking at the organization chart of a large corporation, apportioning one chapter to each of its main divisions.

In this book, we don't take the topical approach. That approach has virtues, but also some significant limitations. First, whether intended or not, it obscures what is common and accentuates what is distinctive in each of the areas that are covered separately. Business ethics emerges less as a unified study of the ethical aspects of doing business and more as an aggregation of particular contexts connected only because they have "something to do with" business. In effect, it says to the marketing major, for example, "Pay special attention to the marketing chapter; the others, not so much." Second, it makes spectators of readers who are not legislators or C-level executives of large, publicly traded corporations. Business ethics, in this approach, is too often about what *someone else* ought to do, rather than what *everyone* ought to do when doing business.

Instead of getting bogged down in topical division and the top-down approach, we will look at the moral features of business that recur across topical areas. We will stress the considerations that bear on business people whether they be corporate functionaries, principals in family businesses, or solo entrepreneurs who do it all, end to end. So, for example, in chapter 2, "What Is Business?," we seek to identify business ethics's object, to say what it is that unifies the functional areas of business and to distinguish business from other forms of human activity. In other words, we focus the inquiry by saying what business is and, of equal importance, what it is not. Business is not "what we do to make money." We do engage in business to make money, but only *some* of the ways we go about making money involve doing business.

In chapter 3, "Ethics as Method," we lay out a particular conception of what it is to "do" ethics, of what it means to engage in applied ethics, and of how this activity is both connected to and distinct from the activity of creating ethical theory. However, the focus of the chapter is what it means to be personally ethical. We do this for two main reasons. First, the bulk of discussion in other business ethics texts focuses on what it means for a business *firm* to be ethical. "Ethical" or "unethical" are evaluative adjectives applied to institutions. The acting human person is too often obscured by the institution in the discussion. Second, we focus on what it is to be personally ethical because we want to present an integrated conception of the ethical business person. An ethical business person is first and foremost an ethical *person*. Her ethical character doesn't stop when the transaction is complete, when the work day is over, or when the vacation starts. To the contrary, her ethical integrity is a defining feature of her life in all its venues and activities.

In chapter 4, "Business Ethics," we draw on the conclusions of chapters 2 and 3 to advance an account of applied ethics and to say how that account applies to business. Appealing to John Stuart Mill's concept of secondary moral principles, we argue that applied ethics is more about identifying good action-guiding principles than about constructing justificatory frameworks. Building on the idea from chapter 2 that business is, at root, a transaction-seeking and transaction-executing practice, and the idea from chapter 3 that overcoming narcissism is fundamental to forming virtuous character, we argue that business ethics is a matter of treating those with whom one does business both as loci of moral value and as responsible agents. In other words, the ethical business person negotiates a path between treating others as objects of predation and treating others as objects of paternalism.

In Chapter 5, "Trust and Truth," we identify the first of the recurrent features of ethical business practice. Business is interactive human engagement. At its most fundamental level, it involves making representations to other people (the truth part) and acting in reliance on their representations (the trust part). This is true whether the business context is sales, advertising, or managing people in organizations. All involve inducing others to rely and relying on others to make good their promises. We argue for both the necessity of truth-telling and the limits of truth-telling in business.

In Chapter 6, "Competition," we observe that competitive activities are important arenas for acquiring and becoming habituated to the virtues. Business competition is in ways similar to, but also distinct from, athletic competition and battle or war. Competition by its nature exerts a form of psychological pressure capable of both motivating people to do great things and encouraging them to lose their sense of proportion about what is competed for. Just as a virtue is a mean between two deficient extremes, the key to ethical competition is to find a way to harness its benefits without competition becoming your master.

In Chapter 7, "Partiality and Impartiality: Loyalty and Its Limits," we observe that although theories of ethical justification are constituted by norms of impartiality, the duties underwritten by them often call on us to exercise partiality on behalf of some as opposed to others. Most business roles are constituted by a mixture of duties to be partial and duties to be impartial. For example, a financial planner at a full-service stock brokerage may be duty-bound to be impartial among all comers in seeking out new customers. So, no potential customer has a claim to becoming a customer that is superior to that of any other potential customer. However, the financial planner may also be duty-bound to favor the interests of a customer over the interests of others in the project of managing that customer's investments. Although in business one often has a duty to be partial, that duty doesn't constitute a moral blank check on how we treat others who are not objects of our partiality. What are the distinguishing features of situations that call for acting impartially? What are the features of situations demanding that one be partial? How are the demands of partiality and impartiality reconciled?

Although at first it may not seem so, Chapter 8, "Work-Life Balance," continues this theme. It asks what is the relationship between work (constituted to some degree by loyalty) and the rest of one's life (constituted by relationships with others that demand loyalty). Work offers the principal means by which we develop character. However, like competition, it can malform us if we don't keep its demands in balance with other things of value. Is working out the proper relationship between work and the rest of your life a matter of determining which of the components of one's life is more important than the others? Is there instead a way to approach this question that harmonizes the components without resorting to such a ham-fisted solution? Does the lack of leisure threaten one's character and integrity in the same way that the pursuit of leisure to the exclusion of work almost certainly does?

Chapter 9, "Big Business and the Global Marketplace," addresses the ethical aspects of business that emerge with scale. Large-scale businesses may be large organizationally, financially, geographically, or in some other way. However, all of those ways raise the same basic question: How does the integrated personality maintain his integrity in an enterprise whose size insulates him from the effects of his actions and some or most of the people they affect? When our actions are far removed from those they affect, it is tempting not to view those people as loci of moral worth or as responsible agents. When one fails to view them as loci of moral worth, they become mere means to our ends. When one fails to view them as responsible agents, one's intentions may be benevolent, but that benevolence takes the form of an unwarranted paternalism. This is especially true in the case of transnational business.

Historically, "international business ethics" has been consumed by two types of questions. First, when they are in conflict, ought "home" country or "host" country norms prevail? Second, is the globalization of business something we ought to acquiesce in or resist? We take a different approach. With respect to globalization, the first thing to acknowledge is that it has already happened and has been happening since at least 1492. Consequently, the question isn't, "Should we or shouldn't we?," but instead "How does the *fact* that ours is a global marketplace bear on what we ought to do when we're doing business?"

In Chapter 10, "The Role of Leadership," we take up the sources of ethical initiative. We commonly use the word *leadership* in two senses. In one sense, it refers to top-down tone-setting by people in positions of authority. In another sense, it refers to leading by example. In the first sense, only the team captain is a leader. In the second sense, even the rookie can be a leader. Whichever sense one uses, leadership is what makes an organization an organization. Consequently, leadership cannot help but bear on the character of each person who makes up the organization. Leadership is thus inseparable from ethics.

Use

The chapters of this book stand alone but are unified by a common approach. They each focus on the individual acting person and what it means to have character and integrity when doing business. Consequently, we believe, as in Rachels's original text, that you can profitably read the whole book or just the chapters that pique your interest. You can read them in the order presented or in an order that makes more sense to you, given your interests or the concepts you wish to highlight.

NOTES

1. Ayn Rand, "Philosophy: Who Needs It," in her essay collection, *Philosophy: Who Needs It* (New York: Signet, 1984), pp. 1–11.
2. Al Gini, *Why It's Hard to Be Good* (New York: Routledge, 2006), p. 21.

3. Simon Blackburn, *Being Good: A Short Introduction to Ethics*, 2nd Ed. (New York: Oxford University Press, 2003).

4. James Rachels, *The Elements of Moral Philosophy*, 4th Ed. (New York: McGraw-Hill, 2003), p. 11.

5. Raymond C. Baumhart, *An Honest Profit: What Businessmen Say about Ethics in Business* (New York: Holt, Rinehart and Winston, 1968), p. xv.

6. L. Trevino, M. Brown, "Managing to Be Ethical: Debunking Five Business Ethics Myths," *Academy of Management Executive* 18 (2004): 69–83.

7. Ed Soule, "Managerial Moral Strategies: In Search of a Few Good Principles," *Academy of Management Review* 27(1) (2002): 114–24.

2

WHAT IS BUSINESS?

The American system of ours, call it Americanism, call it Capitalism, call it what you like, gives each and every one of us a great opportunity if we only seize it with both hands and make the most of it.

—Al Capone, successful gangster and business person

It takes thirty years to make an overnight success.

—Eddie Cantor

I find in running a business that the best results come from letting high grade people work unencumbered.

—Warren Buffett

INTRODUCTION

How will I make my way in the world? That is humanity's fundamental question. Providing for your sustenance is the most basic of human needs. One way to make your way in the world—the way everyone does initially—is as a dependent of others. That is, one way to secure your sustenance is by consuming another person's surplus production. Children are sustained by the surplus of their parents.

In old age, that relationship may be reversed. For some—the physically infirm, the mentally defective, the ne'er do well—dependency on the surplus production of others may be a lifelong condition.

Depending on another's productivity is only one way to provide for your sustenance. If not as a dependent of others, how else can you do it? One way is by selling your labor—lending your productive capacity to the projects of others in return for wages. You might work for a not-for-profit organization, like a charitable foundation; your wages paid by donations from well-meaning others. You might work for a government agency; your wages paid by taxes collected from others. You might work for a private, for-profit firm; your wages paid by revenues from the sale of that firm's goods or services to others. Or you might take a different tack. Rather than depending on another person's surplus production or laboring for others' projects, you might seek to live by the profits that come from devising, producing, and selling a good or service yourself. Rather than collecting a fixed wage, you could "eat what you kill." That is, you might go into business.

FIRST TRY: BUSINESS IS WHAT CORPORATIONS DO

What is business? It seems like a silly question because we all know (or at least, think we know) what business is: Business is what *corporations* do. Corporations are easy to identify. American Express, Coca-Cola, General Electric, Home Depot, McDonalds, Microsoft, and Verizon, for example, are among the largest of large corporations. Their shares are traded on public stock exchanges and held by people the world over. So, to understand what business is we need only observe what they do. And whatever they do is business.

Problem: Not All Corporations Do Business

This seemingly straightforward understanding of business gets wrecked on the rocks of two basic problems. First, not all corporations are business corporations. In addition to business corporations there are, for example, municipal corporations and not-for-profit corporations. Municipal corporations are formed to establish local government entities, like cities.[1]

Not-for-profit corporations are formed most frequently to promote charitable endeavors. It would be wrong to say that whatever municipal corporations do (for example, issue parking citations) is business. Similarly, it would be wrong to say that whatever not-for-profit corporations do (for example, conduct adult literacy programs) is business.

Problem: Not All Business Doers Are Corporations

The second, and perhaps the most obvious, problem is that not all business doers are corporations. In addition to the business corporations we are familiar with, business doers include sole proprietorships, general partnerships, and limited partnerships.[2] Sole proprietorships are business firms wholly owned by an individual person. That person is liable for all debts of the business venture and has a claim on all its profits. General partnerships are business firms owned by two or more persons, called general partners. Each general partner is liable for all debts of the business venture, and each has a claim on an agreed-upon share of the profits. Limited partnerships are business firms owned by one or more general partners and one or more limited partners. Limited partners share in the profits of the business venture but have no managerial role. Unlike general partners, they are liable for the debts of the business venture only to the extent of the capital they contribute to it.

There are also business corporations whose ownership shares aren't traded on public exchanges. These may be vast enterprises whose shares could be traded publicly if management wanted to take the firm public. For example, Cargill is a vast agricultural enterprise. Koch Industries is in a variety of businesses from commodities trading to mining, oil refining, ranching, and forest products. They are two of the largest corporations in the world, but you won't find their share prices quoted in the *Wall Street Journal* or the ticker on CNBC. Other business corporations may be smaller firms whose ownership shares are held by only a few family members or managers. Indeed, most of the world's business corporations are like this. These firms are incorporated so their owners can enjoy the limited liability and tax advantages the corporate form provides, but they are otherwise nothing like the vast, multinational enterprises we think of when we hear the word *corporation*.

Cooperatives are business doers, too. In cooperatives, ownership shares are not held by investors but instead by those who bear some *other* substantial relationship to the business venture. There are worker cooperatives, customer cooperatives, and supplier cooperatives. Worker cooperatives are business firms owned by some or all their employees. Law firms are essentially worker cooperatives owned by some of their lawyers (partners), who employ other lawyers on a contract basis (associates). Customer cooperatives are business firms owned by those who buy the firm's products. Ace Hardware, for example, is owned by the proprietors of the independent hardware stores that are its franchisees. Supplier cooperatives are business firms owned by some or all who sell their products to the firm as inputs to the business venture. Ocean Spray, for example, is a marketing cooperative owned by the farmers who supply it with fruit to make juices.

So, if not all corporations are business doers and not all business doers are corporations, then business is not simply whatever corporations do. Changing the initial account of what business is to "business is what business doers do" shows the poverty of this approach. We need to know what business *is* in order to identify who is doing it.

SECOND TRY: BUSINESS IS WHAT ORGANIZATIONS DO

Some may try to slip this punch by saying that business is what *organizations* do. While this escapes the problem of self-reference that dooms "business is what business doers do," it runs aground for the same reasons. First, there are organizations that don't do business. A ladies bridge club is an organization. But if its activities consist of scheduling and publicizing the next game, and then playing bridge at the appointed place and time, that isn't very much like doing business.

Second, there are business doers who aren't organizations. Some solo entrepreneurs sell their services, perform them, accept payment, pay their expenses, and keep the profits left over. In Chicagoland, where the authors live, The Fix-It Guy is a home appliance repair man. He advertises his services on the Internet and takes calls on his iPhone. He drives to the homes of people with broken appliances, performs repairs, takes payment, and then moves on to the next job. His entire operation consists of himself, a truck, some tools, and his iPhone. The Fix-It Guy is undoubtedly doing business, but he is not an organization and doesn't have recourse to one when doing business.

Nouns versus Verbs

The problem is that we don't look around when thinking of business. We don't look down the street at McGillicuddy's Bakery or across the way at the Osaka sushi bar. We only look up when looking at the business world—at American Express, Coca-Cola, General Electric, Home Depot, McDonalds, Microsoft, and Verizon. Habitually, whether because of our education, the media, or some other force, we look right past the vibrant commercial activity going on all around us. We seem to see *business* only when looking at a megacorporation.

What should be clear from this discussion is that we use the word *business* predominantly in two senses. One sense refers to an *entity*, the business firm. The other sense refers to an *activity*, doing business. One sees business as a noun. The other sees it as a verb. So far, we've tried to understand business by focusing on the noun form. That effort raised more questions than it answered. The path to progress in understanding business may be instead to focus on the verb.

This approach isn't strange. Think about it in other contexts; for example, medicine and law. You would be hard-pressed to recognize a hospital as a *hospital* without observing that medicine is practiced there. The fact that it is an organization supporting medical practice *makes* it a hospital. Similarly, legal practice makes a law firm a *law* firm. The fact that it is an organization supporting legal practice *makes* it a law firm. The nouns (hospital, law firm) are defined by the verbs (practicing medicine, practicing law) they support. If that is correct, then it seems that the practice an organization supports makes it the kind of organization it is. To identify a business organization, perhaps we need to identify the characteristics of the practice it supports.

THIRD TRY: BUSINESS AS A VERB

Executing Exchange Transactions

Although we have a habit of reaching directly for the business entity, it pays to resist it for a moment. We have right under our hats an intuitive grasp of what it is to *do* business. People *do* business when they *transact* or *trade*. You engage in trade by relinquishing some property rights and acquiring other property rights by means of exchange with another person. You relinquish two dollars to acquire a two-pack of Pilot G2 gel pens at Staples. Staples relinquishes a Pilot two-pack to acquire two dollars. You have each relinquished and acquired—or exchanged—property rights. So business is, at its most fundamental level, the activity of executing exchange transactions. This seems intuitively plausible. If Staples didn't engage in exchange transactions, it wouldn't be a business firm.

Identifying Opportunities

We don't do business only when we are executing exchange transactions. Exchange transaction opportunities don't always present themselves immediately and transparently. We have to seek them out. It may be as simple as finding a convenient vendor who sells what you want to buy—like two-packs of Pilot G2 gel pens. It may be as complex as identifying potential customers for a product yet unmade. The inventors of the first "home computer" (a forerunner to the modern PC) were initially at a loss for whom to market it to. When asked for a practical application of their product, their first idea was that housewives would keep recipes on it.[3] Needless to say, a recipe file costing hundreds or thousands of dollars didn't sound like wise investment, and the earliest home computers found a market mostly with electronics hobbyists. It wasn't until the invention of spreadsheet software—forerunners to Microsoft Excel—that the vast market for personal computers developed. That software offered cost savings to business firms doing their books by hand that made the personal computer a must-have business machine.

Finding transactional opportunities requires alertness and imagination about how best to make them happen. Knowing *that* there are people who will pay money to use a personal computer is only part of the challenge. You must conceive a business model they will respond to: Will customers buy or rent? Will software be included or purchased separately? You have to imagine and create both the product and the customer.

When Sony created the Walkman, the first fully portable consumer device capable of playing music you choose, they weren't responding to a preexisting demand. No one was clamoring for a way to play audiocassette tapes while walking, biking, or running. Indeed, the Walkman was lampooned in the press for its lack of a recording function (like most cassette players of the time) and Sony's bold optimism in producing thirty thousand of them for market in 1979. No cassette player had sold more than fifteen thousand units at the time.[4] But Sony was imagining a customer—one who likes to walk, likes to listen to music, and *might* like to do those things together. People responded, adopting the lifestyle that Sony imagined and the Walkman made possible.

The Walkman was the portable music player to have for nearly two decades (first in cassette and later in CD form)—until Apple imagined another customer. Looking at portable music players at the dawn of the twenty-first century, Apple saw an inherent limitation. The Walkman and devices like it were dependent on physical media. You could only listen to as many cassette tapes or CDs as it was convenient for you to carry. Although early flash-based MP3 players weren't tied to physical media, they could only hold about as much music as a CD could. Moreover, you could only listen to your music in the order it was pressed onto the CD or copied onto the flash player. Apple imagined a customer who would like to listen to any song in her music collection at any time, wherever she happened to be. They created the hard-drive-based iPod to cater to this imagined consumer. Although the iPod, too, was lampooned by the media when it came to market in 2001, people responded. They stopped carrying physical media or low-capacity flash players and adopted the lifestyle Apple CEO Steve Jobs had imagined. Today people take the iPod for granted as *the* way to listen to portable music.

These stories illustrate that business is an activity, an *entrepreneurial* activity. Entrepreneurs don't wait passively for customers to come to them. They aren't order takers. Entrepreneurs are alert to possibilities and imagine lifestyles that people may be attracted to, once the possibility is presented to them. Because alertness and imagination are critical to creating opportunities to execute transactions, business is not just a transaction-executing, but also a transaction-seeking, practice.

Bargaining and Negotiation

Although transactions are the soul of business activity, they are not the whole of it. In order to engage in a business transaction the parties must settle what they are transacting for. What is to be exchanged for what? This they accomplish through bargaining and negotiation. Business people, particularly those who engage in commercial transactions, must negotiate the terms on which they will sell their products. They must negotiate with suppliers the terms on which they will buy the inputs used to make their products. They must negotiate the terms on which suppliers will deliver them. If they hire labor to make their products, they must negotiate with employees terms on which they will enter into or continue employment. Exchange transactions don't execute themselves. Negotiation is their prologue. Indeed, negotiation is probably the fundamental skill of the successful business person.[5]

Our common experience with retail consumer transactions makes it easy to overlook this aspect of business. In most retail settings, the merchant announces a take-it-or-leave-it price and the consumer either buys (takes it) or refuses (leaves it). To most people, this is the opposite of bargaining and negotiation. But is it? The merchant proposes a transaction at her announced price and the consumer either rejects or accepts it. Where the consumer rejects, the merchant has the option—although not the obligation—to propose a transaction at a different price or on different terms. Advertised specials—20% off this Monday only! Buy one, get one free! Discounts for senior citizens!—aren't just ways for merchants to be nice to some or all of their customers. They are new proposals to potential buyers who have rejected the existing offer. In other words, merchants and their potential customers are engaged in an ongoing, I-propose-you-dispose negotiation.

If you think that's a strange form of negotiation, consider a different forum: politics. Under the U.S. Constitution, federal law is made by both houses of Congress passing a bill (the proposal) and the president signing (accepting) it. The president also has also the option of vetoing (rejecting) the bill, in which case it doesn't become law. In other words, Congress proposes, the president disposes. Of course, the president can indicate to Congress what kinds of bills he is likely to sign as a way to get more favorable proposals from Congress. Congressional delegations can indicate to the president what kinds of bills they are willing to pass. This process looks like bargaining in the more familiar form. But note that consumers and merchants do this, too. The bold customer who tells the shopkeeper that she'd buy at half off is like the president telling Congress what bills he'll sign. With the advent of the Internet, two-way communication between sellers and buyers is commonplace. In a company-hosted Internet forum, for example, customers offer their preferences about prices, the company's mix of products, and their features. In other words, they're indicating the kinds of products they are willing to buy and the prices at which they'll buy them. These are just offers and counteroffers—bargaining and negotiation at the retail level.

Bargaining and negotiation require identifying someone to transact with. Business people engage in advertising as an overture to negotiation, asking potential transactors to identify themselves. An advertisement announces your availability to negotiate over transactions of a certain kind. It may communicate a proposal (in which case it is an act of negotiation, as well). Alternatively, it may merely indicate one's willingness to entertain proposals. Either way, advertising is a central practice of business.

Self-Sustaining Transactional Activity

Transactions are sought and executed not for their own sake, but in pursuit of an end. Not all ends sought through exchange transactions are business ends. Imagine a medical clinic that solicits donations from concerned citizens, buys medical supplies, and offers free health care to the indigent. It is transaction-seeking and transaction-executing insofar as it buys medical supplies, but we are rightly reluctant to characterize its activities as business. That is because the medical clinic doesn't try to sustain itself through its exchange transactions. Instead, it tries to sustain itself through donations. Without them, the medical clinic couldn't buy supplies and offer free health care. The medical clinic is not a business venture, but a charitable endeavor.

In a similar vein, consider the viewer-supported public television station. Like the free medical clinic, it seems to rely on monetary gifts to sustain itself and so is not engaged in business. Indeed, public television donors are usually called sustaining members—suggesting that it is their donations, not the transactional activities of the public television station, that are intended to sustain it. But these sustaining pledges are not always straightforward gifts. When a donation of $100 nets the viewer a *Best of Peter, Paul & Mary* CD, this seems at first blush like a sale—a transaction—rather than a gift. If every donation garners the donor something in return from the public television station, isn't it sustaining itself through exchange transactions?

Note, however, that the donor would not pay *just anyone* $100 for the CD. If the donor's local Barnes & Noble charges $100 for the CD, which is priced at $20 on Amazon, the donor would be disinclined to pay $100 to Barnes & Noble. In other words, the donor doesn't value the *Best of Peter, Paul & Mary* CD at $100. If all she wants is a *Best of Peter, Paul & Mary* CD, she does better to buy it at Amazon. She pays $100 because she values the public television station's service and wishes to support it. The public television station is not in the business of selling music CDs. If it were, it would soon be out of business—not least for its limited selection of music titles. Instead, the public television station is soliciting donations, just like the free medical clinic, above. The donations it solicits are interesting because they bundle two interactions between the donor and the public television station. One interaction is a $100 gift to the public television station from the donor. The other is a lesser gift to the donor—a token of appreciation from the public television station. The public television station isn't doing business because viewer donations, not exchange transactions, are intended to sustain it. It is a not-for-profit enterprise providing a public service.

In a different vein, consider hobbies. Some hobbies may involve much transaction-seeking and transaction-executing activity. One of the authors collects vintage fountain pens as a hobby. Vintage fountain pen collecting involves much buying, selling, and bartering of pens and parts. Each purchase, each sale, and each bartered exchange is a transaction both sought and executed. However, we are rightly reluctant to call the vintage fountain pen hobbyist's activities business. His transaction-seeking and transaction-executing behavior is usually not intended to sustain itself. Usually, the hobbyist raises money from other sources—his job—to support his continued participation in the hobby. It is not coincidental that hobbyists talk about their passion as if it were a drug habit—something they have to raise money for in order to continue, despite the ruin it brings to their wallets.

What is missing from the free medical clinic, the public television station, and the hobby that keep them from being business ventures? The answer is transactional activity that is intended to at least pay for itself and, if things go very well, yield more value than was relinquished in making the transactions. In other words, a person, a firm, or an enterprise engages in business by seeking to identify and implement *profitable* sets of transactions. These are transactions that permit continuing transactional activity and perhaps financing other projects, as well. Business is engaging in transactional activities with the intention of making a profit.

The free medical clinic could choose instead to sell medical services and sustain itself through fees charged to its patients. In the long run, it would be able to continue only if the fees at least covered its costs. If it pursued this path, the medical clinic would no longer be a free medical clinic. It would be engaged in business.

Similarly, the public television station could choose instead to sell commercial airtime or become a subscription-only cable station. It could seek to sustain itself through the revenues generated from selling commercials or subscriptions. In the long run, it would be able to continue only if the commercial or subscription fees at least covered its costs. If it pursued this path, the television station would no longer be a public television station. It would be engaged in business.

Finally, the vintage fountain pen hobbyist could choose instead to use only such money as he generates from buying, selling, and bartering pens to support his activities. In the long run, he would be able to continue only if the revenues of his transactions at least covered their costs. If he pursued this path, he would no longer be a hobbyist. He would be engaged in business.

PURSUIT OF PROFIT

Does this mean that by pursuing the alternative path the medical clinic, the television station, and fountain pen enthusiast would be "just in it for the money"? Does this mean that profits are ends in themselves? No. Profits are the ends of business activity. People seek profits through business activity so they can use those profits to pursue other things. No reasonably reflective person wants money for its own sake. She wants money because it facilitates other projects she values. Consequently, nothing here depends upon the idea that people (even business people) are motivated exclusively, or even primarily, by profit. The idea is that people pursue their objectives through *business*—rather than through other means—when they aim to transact in an intentionally profit-generating (self-sustaining) way. Business is the pursuit and execution of intentionally self-sustaining transactional activity.

With this idea in mind, are all attempts to make a profit business ventures? Consider the plot of the film and Broadway musical, *The Producers*. Max Bialystock, a failed Broadway producer, conspires with his accountant, Leo Bloom, to make lots of money by staging the musical play *Springtime for Hitler*. They choose the play because its loving celebration of *der Führer* makes it certain to fail at the box office. Their scheme is to oversell ownership shares in the musical and pocket the excess money. Then they will skip off to Brazil, secure in the knowledge that when *Springtime for Hitler* fails at the box office no one will audit the books of a so-obviously-failed venture.[6] Bialystock and Bloom ultimately sell 25,000 percent worth of ownership interests in *Springtime for Hitler*, mostly to rich little old ladies seduced by Bialystock's charm. In other words, they sell "full" ownership in the musical production 250 times over (250 x 100% = 25,000%).

The scheme backfires because audiences enjoy *Springtime for Hitler*—as a hilarious *comedy*. The musical's unintended and critically acclaimed success means that Bialystock and Bloom's production owes its investors $250 for every dollar of profit *Springtime for Hitler* makes. Tried for fraud and found "incredibly guilty," Bialystock and Bloom go to prison. There, they organize *Prisoners in Love*, a play starring their fellow convicts. Their plan is to run the same scam again.

The comic genius of *The Producers* aside, it is interesting to consider whether Bialystock and Bloom's scheme is a business venture.

Are Bialystock and Bloom doing business? At first blush, it appears they are. They are certainly portraying it as such to their investors, to their playwright, to the public, and to the actors and director they hire. Moreover, they seem to be trying to sustain themselves through exchange transactions—relinquishing ownership interests in the play in order to acquire the funds they are counting on for their scheme to succeed. They purchase the services of actors, a director, and a playwright to further their scheme. They rent a theater, as well.

But note two things: First, Bialystock and Bloom aren't entering into exchange transactions with their investors. They are selling ownership shares in *Springtime for Hitler* that don't exist. That is, they are feigning exchange transactions in order to accomplish theft. In other words, they are taking something in return for nothing. Bialystock and Bloom acquire without relinquishing what they promise—namely, ownership shares in the production. Second, the exchange transactions that they do engage in—with audiences who buy tickets from Bialystock and Bloom; with actors, a director, and stagehands who sell their labor to Bialystock and Bloom—are not intended to be self-sustaining. Indeed, the whole point of those transactions is to lose money; to undermine the *Springtime for Hitler* production rather than to sustain it. In other words, Bialystock and Bloom aren't doing business. Their fraud is that they are pretending to be doing business in order to fleece the investors who are fooled into thinking they are engaged in business.

CONCLUSION

In summary, the exchange transaction is the soul of business. It is the thing without which there can be no business. Business is first and foremost a transaction-seeking and transaction-executing activity. It is pursued with the intention of executing profitable sets of transactions so the activity can be self-sustaining. Of course, there's more to business than that. In its fullness business is compound, complex, and often confusing. But beneath it all these elements remain. Starting with the exchange transaction and working outward, we see that business is ubiquitous. It is done by many people and firms, not just the large corporations we think of first when we think of business. How you conduct yourself when seeking and executing exchange transactions is the essence of your character as a business person.

NOTES

1. See, e.g., "Municipal Corporation," Answers.com (accessed May 27, 2010, at URL: www.answers.com/topic/municipal-corporation) (text from *West's Encyclopedia of American Law*).

2. See, e.g., "Sole Proprietorship," YourDictionary.com (accessed May 27, 2010, at URL: www.yourdictionary.com/law/sole-proprietorship) (text from *Webster's New World Law Dictionary* [Hoboken, N.J.: Wiley, 2010]); "Partnership," YourDictionary.com (accessed May 27, 2010, at URL: www.yourdictionary.com/law/partnership) (text from *Webster's New World Law Dictionary* [Hoboken, N.J.: Wiley, 2010]).

3. See, e.g., the Wikipedia entry "home computer" (accessed November 16, 2009, at URL: http://en.wikipedia.org/wiki/Home_computer).

4. See Tom Hormby, "The Story behind the Sony Walkman," Low End Mac.com, September 15, 2006 (accessed October 21, 2009, at URL: http://lowendmac.com/orchard/06/sony-walkman-origin.html).

5. See, e.g., Steve Gates, "Time to Take Negotiation Seriously," *Industrial and Commercial Training* 38(5) (2006): 238–41.

6. This isn't as weird as it might sound. Ownership shares in Broadway shows are often marketed to investors as vehicles for generating tax losses they can write off against other income. Although they try to make money, most Broadway shows actually end up losing money, and no one thinks it's strange when they do.

3

ETHICS AS METHOD[1]

The unexamined life is not worth living.

—Socrates

Is it more important to know what makes wrongdoing wrong, or what makes right-doing right?

—One of the authors, in conversation

Reportedly, Winston Churchill once said of a political opponent: "Deep down, there's a lot less there than meets the eye." He was referring, of course, to his opponent's character or lack thereof. And it is just this phenomenon, the absence of character or, more precisely, the possession of a flawed character, that goes a long way to explain the difficulty that so many people have in figuring out what they "ought to do." Aristotle suggested, as did British philosopher G. E. M. Anscombe and many others, that to do ethics properly you must start with what a person needs and must have to flourish and live well—character. For Aristotle the ethical life is grounded on the development and expression of character.

CHARACTER

The root word of *character* is the Greek word for etching or engraving, *charaktêr*. Used originally to signify the marks engraved upon a coin, when applied to human beings *charaktêr* refers to the enduring marks or etched-in factors that have been impressed on our minds, our *psyches*, which include our inborn talents as well as the learned and acquired traits imposed upon us by education and experience. These engravings set us apart, define us, and motivate behavior.

Although much of character is imposed on us by culture, the vagaries of time and place, and the genetic and behavioral influences of our parents, character is also about what a person *chooses* to hold dear, to value, and to believe in. To paraphrase Eleanor Roosevelt, if you want to know what a person values, check their checkbook. If you want to know about a person's character, check their values. And, if you want to know a person's ethics, check their character.

William James believed that the most interesting and important thing about a person, and that which determines one's perspective on the world, is a philosophy of life—the values, ideals, and beliefs we choose to hold dear. They are things we are willing to act for and act on. Values, ideals, and beliefs are the road maps that help us to decipher and explain what James calls the "booming, buzzing confusion" of reality. Our philosophies of life are defined by what we choose to value, and our characters are defined by actually living out what we value. For example, James believes that an honest person experiencing hard times will make every effort to sooner or later honor a debt, but that a dishonest person may never repay a debt even if he possesses more than sufficient resources to do so.

VIRTUE

Virtues are desirable, lived-out behavior traits that are essential for achieving happiness and getting along with others—that is, for living well. According to Aristotle, a virtue is a mean or midpoint between the defect and excess of a character trait. For example, in the sphere of action or feeling involving fear or confidence, the virtue *bravery* is the mean between the defect of *cowardice* and the excess of *rashness*. A cowardly soldier is one who flees or surrenders even when he ought to fight. A rash soldier is one who goes looking for a fight even when it isn't necessary for achieving his military objectives. The brave soldier, by comparison, fights at the right time, for the right objectives, and in the right measure. Unlike the cowardly soldier, he fights even when it is difficult or dangerous for him to do it. Unlike the rash soldier, he retreats when the battle is lost because, as the saying goes, "discretion is the better part of valor." (*Valor* is another word for bravery.) Thus, for Aristotle, bravery is the "golden mean" between cowardice and rashness.

There are more virtues than bravery. For Aristotle, in the sphere of seeking or experiencing pleasure or pain, *temperance* is the virtuous mean between the defect of *insensibility* and the excess of *licentiousness* or *self-indulgence*. In the sphere of getting or spending, *magnificence* is a virtuous mean between *pettiness* and *vulgarity*. In the sphere of honor and dishonor, *pride* is virtuous mean between an *undue humility* and *vanity*.

According to Aristotle, we choose our virtues. By repeatedly acting on them they become second nature, hardening into habit. Virtuous behavior is not accident, mere luck, or a one-time event. A virtuous act is doing the right thing for the right reason, habitually, and on purpose. A person of good character has a constellation of virtues. For him, virtuous action is the rule, not the exception. Thus, acting virtuously is itself a habit. Ethics, explained the late philosopher Robert Solomon, is a question of one's whole character, not just a question of this particular virtue or that.[2]

INTEGRITY

The Romans used a perfect Latin word to describe the quality of a person's character, *integritas*—from which we get the English word *integrity*. Integrity means "the state or quality of being entire or complete." It means soundness, being unimpaired, having all the component pieces fit together and be whole. A person with ethical integrity manifests in action a constellation of virtues that complement and reinforce each other. That person practices self-restraint, self-control, and self-mastery. He is not a slave to his emotions or his passions but is coolheaded and reasonable.

Integrity is not the mere collection of virtues. The concept is qualitative, not quantitative. Integrity means "living coherently," what the Greek stoics called *homologoumenôs zên*—presenting oneself, to oneself and to the world, in a way that is whole and unified, not Janus-faced, fractured, or schizophrenic. Integrity is about personal identity and honor. For the philosopher Bernard Williams, having integrity is acting in accordance with one's identity-conferring commitments—the commitments that you hold so deeply that to act contrary to them would be to give up on who you are. (Think of a time when you may have done something that is such a betrayal and so contrary to character that someone close to you has said, "I don't even know who you are.")

An integrated character does not say one thing and do another. Neither does an integrated character do and say one thing when no one else is around and yet another when others are present. An integrated character is a harmonious, intact, mutually reinforcing whole. Having integrity is something that all morally serious people care about and think important. In both personal relationships and public life, to describe someone as lacking integrity is to offer a damning diagnosis.

> It carries the implication that this individual is not to be relied upon, that in some fundamental way they are not someone who we can, or should, view as being wholly unequivocally there. The foundations of self and character are not sound; the ordering of values is not coherent.[3]

In his 1996 book, *Integrity*, Stephen L. Carter suggests that integrity is a kind of *über*-virtue or "philosophical cement" that contains and coordinates all of one's other virtues and values. Carter understands integrity as having the courage of one's convictions. He suggests that if ethics is living out what we value, then the integrity of a person's character, or lack thereof, is as good a yardstick as any to predict ethical conduct. Carter describes integrity in terms of three characteristics:

1. One must take pains to try to discern right from wrong.
2. One must be willing to shape one's actions in accord with that discernment, even when it is difficult or painful to do so. (As Walter Lippman so eloquently phrased it, "He has honor if he holds himself to an ideal of conduct though it is inconvenient, unprofitable, or dangerous to do so.")
3. One must be willing to acknowledge publicly what one is doing.

In short, a person of integrity must be reflective, steadfast, trustworthy, and whole. "A person of integrity," writes Carter, "is a whole person, a person somehow undivided."[4]

CONSCIENCE

According to *Chicago Tribune* columnist Eric Zorn, a person of character is someone who has a conscience. To most modern ears, says Zorn, the word *conscience* is unfortunately too abstract, ephemeral, and downright old-fashioned to be used in most conventional conversations. What comes to mind, for a lot of people, is the image of a little person sitting on your shoulder who is whispering in your ear and offering advice and judgment on the moral goodness or blameworthiness of your actions. Nevertheless, Zorn argues, even though the word is rarely used, its meaning is neither obsolete or irrelevant.[5]

Conscience is from the Latin *conscire*—to be conscious; to know. It implies care, concern, or at the very least, the recognition of others. One's conscience is not just a nagging, faultfinding, superego cop. Conscience is the ability to reflect on, be sensitive to, evaluate, and make judgments about one's interactions with others. It is not an infallible instinct, an emotional buzzer that can always distinguish between right and wrong. It is not a perfect truth detector. But if we are lucky and not totally lost in the emotional maze of our own narcissism, conscience at the very least forces us to ponder our relationships with others and to make some sort of judgment about what is acceptable or unacceptable behavior in their regard.

If character is living out what we value, conscience is that computer chip that makes judgments and evaluations about when, how, and with whom one's values should be pursued. Conscience requires us to consider others.

Like being virtuous, being a person of conscience is an ongoing activity, not a one-time affair or an episodic experience. Though it may be revealed most readily in high-stakes circumstances or difficult dilemmas, it is practiced in situations both mundane and exceptional, when one is alone and when others are looking on. Thus, ethical character is formed over time and can withstand the test of time. Aristotle reportedly said, "Never judge a person moral until they are dead." He meant that on any given day or moment we make mistakes, we fail, we act in ways we wish we would not. Who among us is without regret or fault? A person's character must be judged in perspective, over time. Character, like a skill or art form, must be practiced to be perfected and maintained. And yet having said this, some mistakes, some actions, some behavior, intended or not, can change our lives and our reputations forever. Vigilance is required!

ETHICS

At its most elemental level, ethics is about critical reflection and analysis. That statement is easy to misunderstand because people use the word *critical* in two different senses. One sense of critical means to attack or to tear down ("He's always critical of me."). That's not the sense we mean here. The other sense of critical means to carefully take apart, to examine, to try to understand, and to make better. It's the sense used in phrases such as "critical thinking." Critical thinking is an attempt to make our ideas and our arguments[6] more logical or more coherent. That's the sense we mean here. Reflecting critically upon something is subjecting it to rational scrutiny, asking and attempting to answer questions about it. Reflecting critically about ethics is subjecting our actions and our principles to rational scrutiny, asking if they are informed by the best reasons. As James Rachels succinctly puts it: "Philosophy, like morality itself, is first and last an exercise in reason—the ideas that should come out on top are the ones that have the best reasons on their sides."[7]

Act-Based versus Character-Based Ethics

Unifying most schools of thought about ethics is the idea that ethics is intimately connected with reason. For virtue ethicists like Aristotle, the virtues can be rationally demonstrated because they are good for man and mankind. Practicing them leads to a flourishing life. Other moral philosophers reject the emphasis on the virtues, believing instead that the proper object of analysis is the action or the decision; actions and decisions, not people or their characters, are good or bad, right or wrong. Rather than listing and describing the virtues we ought to manifest through our actions or decisions, these moral philosophers seek to explain the features of actions or decisions themselves that make them good or bad, right or wrong. Their aim is to articulate a master value or rule that people can use as a recipe to select the best action or decision. In the utilitarian ethics of Jeremy Bentham or John Stuart Mill, for example, actions or decisions are judged by their *consequences* for all affected people. More particularly, an action or decision is good to the extent that it promotes happiness. It is bad to the extent that it brings unhappiness. Utilitarianism is the view that, when choosing among alternatives, a person ought to select the one that maximizes net happiness (happiness minus unhappiness) for all affected people. Call this the Principle of Utility. Utilitarianism's recipe for right action could be expressed this way:

1. Identify the alternatives.
2. For each alternative, add up all the happiness it will bring to affected people and subtract all of the unhappiness it will bring to affected people.

3. Select and perform the alternative that brings the most net happiness (happiness minus unhappiness) or, if none brings net happiness, then the least net unhappiness.

Utilitarianism is the view that happiness is of ultimate moral importance and we ought to do what brings the most happiness.

By contrast, in the duty-based ethics of Immanuel Kant, actions or decisions are judged, at least in part, by the intentions of the actor. According to Kant, the only thing that is completely good in itself is a good will. A good will is one that acts from duty, and not merely in compliance with duty. That raises a natural question: What duties do we have?

To understand the duties we have, we have to understand what makes human beings morally valuable. Human beings have the capacity for rational deliberation and action. That means that we can guide our actions by *reasons*. Whereas other members of the animal kingdom are guided by instinct (the combination genetic inheritances and environmental cues that, for example, make a beaver build a dam), human beings are capable of resisting instinct and acting on the basis of rules and principles that can be given a rational foundation. Because of this ability, human beings are what the philosopher Loren Lomasky calls "project pursuers."[8] We are capable not merely of seeing the world as it is (by the evidence of our senses) but also of imagining it being different (through the application of human action guided by rules and principles). We can imagine it being different in many different ways, and we can use reason to decide which of those ways are worth pursuing. Then we move our bodies and marshal resources in order to make what we imagine real. This aspect of our humanity shows, in the Christian understanding, that we are "made in the image of God" (Genesis 1:27). We are not God, but godlike. Like God, we are capable (albeit in our limited and imperfect way) of creative acts.[9]

According to Kant, this special capacity of ours means that we are capable of governing ourselves by principle. The most basic principle is that we act on the basis of rationally derived, universal law—what Kant calls the Categorical Imperative: Act only on that maxim (read: principle of action) that you can will to be universal law.[10] In other words, if the tables were turned and you would instead be on the receiving end of your proposed principle of action (or if you were an impartial spectator), would you still believe that others in this position ought to act on it? Implied in the Categorical Imperative is *moral equality*, the idea that we are all subject to the moral law and none of us may treat our own as a special case just because it's ours. In other words, the Categorical Imperative forbids one to conclude that it is wrong for *others* to lie, but not for oneself to lie. The Categorical Imperative is, in effect, a secular version of the biblical Golden Rule: "[W]hatever you want men to do to you, do also to them" (Matthew 7:12), "And as ye would that men should do to you, do ye also to them likewise" (Luke 6:31), or, as it is often expressed ordinarily today, "Do unto others as you would have them do to you."

The second principle (also known as the second formulation of the Categorical Imperative) is that one ought to treat humanity, whether yourself or another, as an end in itself and not only as a means.[11] In other words, one ought to respect in all persons the thing that makes them human. Recall that the defining characteristic of human beings and the thing that makes them morally valuable is the capacity for rational deliberation and action. This second principle says that our actions ought to honor and respect this capacity rather than attempt to overcome it or extinguish it. This is why lying is wrong: It is an attempt to circumvent (overcome) the capacity for rational deliberation and action by making others believe and act on things that aren't true. This is also why murder (willful killing without justification) is wrong: It extinguishes life and, with it, the capacity for rational deliberation and action.

In contrast to utilitarianism, Kant's duty-based ethics values respect for humanity rather than happiness-making. Indeed, respecting another person's humanity may make that other person (and others besides) unhappy. Imagine that you go to your grandmother's house every Thanksgiving, and every Thanksgiving she makes turkey that is dry, tough, and flavorless. This Thanksgiving she asks you, "Darling, how's the turkey?" Promoting happiness for all affected people calls for you to tell what we sometimes call a *white lie* (a lie that is well intentioned): "The turkey's great, grandma!" But respecting your grandmother's capacity for rational deliberation and action calls for you to tell her the truth: "The turkey is dry, tough, and flavorless." Why? Because by telling the white lie, you impair your grandmother's capacity for rational deliberation and action. When making the turkey next year, she may take your assurance that her turkey is good as a reason not to explore new recipes and cooking methods—when that's exactly what her turkey needs.

Although it cannot be as easily reduced to a recipe for right action as utilitarianism can, Kant's duty-based ethics shares with utilitarianism a number of basic features:

1. It focuses on the moral character of actions and decisions, rather than of persons.
2. It posits a single, ultimate value (rationality; compare happiness).
3. It articulates a small number of principles that, when applied to decisions or actions, aspire to yield a single, determinate answer about what you ought to do (the two formulations of the Categorical Imperative; compare the Principle of Utility).

Kant's duty-based ethics calls on us to act on the basis of duties to respect the essential humanity of ourselves and others.

So far in this book, we have written mostly about character and the virtues that make up good character. That we have done for two reasons. First, *people* are the authors of actions. The moral character of an action cannot help but be an indication of the moral character of the person who performed it. Second, by splitting off the person from her actions, act-based ethics invites the self-deception that one can be a "good person" even when doing bad things—the badness infects the action, not the person performing it. That form of self-deception is attractive because we as human beings assess personal character as readily as we assess personal beauty. But the reality is that our actions form our character to ourselves and others. And our character is known by the actions we perform. Consequently, for the balance of the book, we will focus on how actions manifest good character. We may draw on act-based ethics on occasion for illustrative purposes, but our main concern will be what a life of good character and conscience consists of.

The Force of Habit

A virtuous person acts rightly, for the right reasons, habitually, and on purpose. Her actions are informed by and manifest the cluster of virtues her character possesses. The most important word in this description of the virtuous person is *habit*. People acquire their virtues (or their vices) through practice and repetition—the same way a baseball player acquires his skills. In the beginning, the budding shortstop needs careful and concentrated effort to position himself properly for turning a double play. Through practice and repetition, he comes to recognize double-play situations immediately and to position himself almost automatically. The skills learned by concentrated effort and repeated practice harden into habit. They become second nature. As it is for the shortstop, so, too, for the virtuous person. A person becomes brave, for example, by putting herself in fearful circumstances and emulating what brave people do. Through practice and repetition, what once required careful and concentrated effort—suppressing her fears, standing firm, betraying no weakness—hardens into habit. In fearful circumstances, she acts bravely as if by second nature.

This emphasis on habit may seem to contradict the earlier emphasis on reason. After all, if one acts habitually it seems he isn't acting on reason. Indeed, one of the attractions of a good habit is that, once acquired, you don't have to think about it directly. However, habit and reason are reconciled in the *selection* virtues we hope to acquire through practice. A budding football player hopes to emulate Ray Lewis, a linebacker known for his considerable skill but more so for his relentless effort, determination, and leadership. (Few football announcers can say ten words about Lewis without calling him a "warrior.") On the field, Lewis is a *role model*. His actions manifest the ideal virtues of a football player and a leader. By contrast, although he is a highly talented wide receiver, Randy Moss is known equally well for his unwillingness to put in his best effort on every down. Moss plays hard when the ball is coming to him, but he gives less effort when he is a decoy or a blocker. His considerable talent was sought by multiple football teams that were later happy to part with him once his half-heartedness surfaced. The budding football player admires Moss's talent but would be foolish to emulate him. On the field, Moss is no role model and no leader. He is a talented but temperamental prima donna. In selecting a player whose virtues he hopes to acquire through practice, the budding football player *reasons* that he will be a better football player by emulating Lewis. Whatever talents the budding football player possesses, they will be put to better use and have greater effect if he approaches the game like Lewis does rather than the way Moss does. Reasonably, he seeks to acquire Lewis's virtues by adopting his habits (for example, play every down like the game depends on it) rather than Moss's.

The history of philosophy is replete with explanations of why it is hard to be good. But when push comes to shove, the root problem of ethics is found at the heart of the human condition. One need not be a scholar of Thomas Hobbes's work or an admirer of Herbert Spencer's to recognize that we are by nature self-absorbed creatures. In the language of virtue ethics we are *habitually* self-centered and self-absorbed—in a word, narcissistic. Though we (almost) all disavow narcissism and are put off by those who exhibit it, we find it too easy to be excessively self-regarding and hard to be even reasonably other-regarding. That is because we see the world—literally—through our own eyes only. We see it through others' eyes, if at all, only metaphorically. Seeing the world through others' eyes demands an affirmative act of imagination, whereas seeing our own point of view is as easy as opening our eyes. In other words, narcissism is an easy habit to form but a hard habit to break.

NARCISSISM

The term *narcissism* or *narcissistic personality type* is not often used in philosophical circles, but perhaps it should be. As a concept, narcissism neatly encapsulates the dark side of why it is so hard to get free of the shadow of self.

According to the *Synopsis of Psychiatry*, persons with narcissistic personality disorder are characterized by a heightened sense of self-importance and grandiose feelings that they are unique—in the true, singular sense of the term.[12] They consider themselves special and expect special treatment. They always want their own way and are frequently ambitious—often desirous of fame and fortune. Their relationships with others are fragile, shallow, and limited. Unable to empathize, they feign sympathy for others only to achieve their own selfish ends. Interpersonal exploitation is commonplace.

A narcissistic individual's entire self is devoted to the pursuit of personal pleasure and self-gratification, with little or no concern for the wants or needs of others. Narcissists are not necessarily vain in a cosmetic sense—demanding the trendiest clothing, the latest car, and plastic surgery to remove every wrinkle and droop—but, cosmologically speaking, the world as they understand it begins and revolves around them. Narcissists create for themselves a self-contained, self-serving worldview, which rationalizes anything done on their behalf and requires justification on no other grounds.

Some of the key methods and behaviors that narcissistic personality types, and those of us locked into our own selfish concerns, implement in order to insulate and isolate themselves include the following.

Instant Gratification

One of the more fundamental reasons why a lot of us, narcissistic types and otherwise, are unable to be sufficiently concerned with ethical considerations is our tendency to overvalue present gratification and to undervalue future benefits and goods. The ability to defer gratification is one of the best measurements of emotional and ethical maturity. Living "in the moment," the emotionally and ethically immature tend to dismiss the past because it is no more and give no thought to the future, because it has not yet arrived. That view is impoverished because it lacks perspective—especially on the nature of the moment in which one aims to live. Reality is the "moment," but only as it comes from the past and leads up to the future. All three temporal dimensions (past, present, future) must be considered and valued in order to develop a consistent and ethically attuned character.

Lack of Moral Imagination

If ethics stirs us beyond the numbness of self, then ethical decision making requires us to look beyond the immediate moment and beyond personal needs, desires, and wants. It calls on us to imagine the possible consequences of our decisions and actions on the self and others. In its most elemental sense, moral imagination is about foreseeing outcomes in our interactions with others, for ourselves *and* others. Think of moral imagination as a virtual dress rehearsal that allows us to examine and appraise different courses of action in order to determine the morally best thing to do.

According to a number of prominent philosophers, it is not always ignorance of moral principles that causes moral ineptitude; sometimes it is the inability to imagine and be sympathetic to the needs, passions, and interests of others. At its core, to sympathize is to place myself in another's situation, "not because of how that situation might affect me, but rather as if I were that person in that situation."[13] Moral imagination allows us to be self-reflective, to step back from our situation and see it from another point of view. In taking such a perspective, a person tries to look at the world and herself from the point of view of another reasonable person—one not solely absorbed with self. This trans-positional perspective has been called "a disengaged view from somewhere" and involves deliberating over questions like:

1. What would a reasonable person judge is the right thing to do?
2. Could one defend this decision publicly?
3. What kind of precedent does this decision set? Would one want it repeated, made into law?
4. Is this decision or action necessary?
5. Is this the least worst option?[14]

What moral imagination suggests, and what narcissistic types are rarely disposed to do, is that in order to make an ethical decision, you have to determine: What's at stake? What are the issues? Who else is involved? And, what are the alternatives? Moral imagination allows the possibility of addressing these questions from a perspective that considers both self and others.

Callousness, Carelessness, and Habit

Narcissistic types are not necessarily cruel or mean or evil, but rather they are serenely unconcerned or indifferent to others. They are hardened to the plight or needs of others. It's not so much that self-absorbed, narcissistic types are consciously unethical; rather, they are thoughtless and, in reality, unconscious of others. In fact, they may be genuinely amoral (without moral concern) in regard to others. In time, of course, callousness, carelessness, and self-absorbed indifference progress from simple behavior traits to habits, and eventually to a way of life that influences if not totally dictates our moral worldview and the choices we make regarding others.

Søren Kierkegaard said that "subjectivity is the starting point of ethics." But subjectivity is neither the end point nor the only point of ethics. Starting from the self, ethics proceeds with the recognition of others as an integral part of developing a virtuous character. Ethics is always about self in the context of others. Ethics means we must be open to the "voice of others." For feminist psychologist Carol Gilligan, caring for others, being responsive to others, being ethical, begins with standing outside of the needs of self and "talking and listening to others."

Business ethicist Elaine Sternberg and theologian Frank Griswald have given us two of the more felicitous definitions of ethics. According to Sternberg, "Ethics is about how you conduct yourself every day, every time." Griswald avers that, "Ethics is about the rules we chose to live by once we decide we want to live together." What both of these definitions emphasize is that ethics is an ongoing task. Ethical character is formed by decisions and actions both large and small. Ethics is something we *do* and do often, whether we think we're doing it or not. Ethics is a consequence of the inescapability of decision. Even when we try to avoid making a decision, we often can't. Most moral dilemmas do not allow us the luxury of neutrality. Moral virtues are rarely cultivated by the act of fence-sitting. In the words of Harvey Cox, "Not to decide, is to decide."

Why Be Moral?

The social, other-regarding part of ethics is hard for some to accept (at least, intellectually) due to the force of one basic question: "Why should one do what is right when doing so is not to one's advantage?" Clearly, it is not always instrumentally rational and personally advantageous to do the right thing. In fact, people are credited with high moral character or are called heroes specifically and especially on the grounds of having done what is right even when it is contrary to their own interest. However, philosopher Philippa Foot argues that morality pays over the course of a life because the alternative, a life of calculation and deception, takes away more in lifelong psychological pressure than it yields in an accumulation of momentary advantages.[15]

The point is, if a person wants to be shown that it is always to one's advantage and that one's life will invariably be better (or, at least, not made worse) by practicing moral virtue, we doubt if this demand can always be met. Perhaps the only response to this question is a burden-shifting one. It was Aristotle who fathered the notion that at the foundation of morals lies the principle that if morality is to be argued about at all, then the onus of justification lies upon those who propose to deny it.

CONCLUSION

Good ethical character is manifest in the overarching virtues of integrity and conscience. Like all virtues, they are acquired through practice and repetition. That is because genuine virtues are habits. The virtues that make up good character are often hard habits to form and easy habits to break, especially when it comes to the other-regarding part of good character. That is because narcissism is an easy habit to form and a hard habit to break. Though they are hard to acquire, the virtues are nonetheless worth acquiring because they lead to the kind of happiness that comes only from a fully integrated personality. Whether out of lassitude, lechery, or the accumulation of bad habits, too many of us find it hard, if not impossible, to recognize and respond to moral dilemmas and their impact on others. We have forgotten a fundamental Socratic lesson: The goal of life is not to escape death, suffering, or inconvenience. The goal is to escape doing wrong, and living well with others.

NOTES

1. Portions of this chapter are drawn from Al Gini and Alexei M. Marcoux, *Case Studies in Business Ethics*, 6th Ed. (Upper Saddle River, N.J.: Pearson Prentice Hall, 2009).

2. Robert C. Solomon, *A Handbook for Ethics* (Orlando, Fla.: Harcourt Brace, 1996), pp. 83–88.

3. "Integrity," Routledge Encyclopedia of Philosophy Online, (accessed February 12, 2010, at URL: www.rep.routledge.com/article/L134?ssid=1231289591&n=1#).

4. Stephen L. Carter quoted in Gilbert Meilaender, "Integral or Divided?," *First Things*, (May 1996): 49–71.

5. Eric Zorn, "'Conscience': Old-Fashioned but Not Obsolete," *Chicago Tribune*, Tempo Section, 2 (May 23, 2002).

6. *Argument* is another word we use in two different senses. One sense refers to a heated disagreement between people. Another sense refers to a collection of logically related reasons designed to support a point.

7. Christopher Phillips, *Socrates Café* (New York, W. W. Norton, 2001), pp. 2, 3.

8. Loren Lomasky, *Persons, Rights, and the Moral Community* (New York: Oxford University Press, 1990).

9. One way to understand Kant's project is as an attempt to provide a secular foundation for Christian ethics. Without excluding God, Kant wanted reason, rather than revelation, to be the basis of ethical decision making and behavior.

10. See, e.g., Immanuel Kant, *Groundwork of the Metaphysic of Morals*, H. J. Paton, trans. (New York: Harper & Row, 1964; originally published 1785), p. 89.

11. Ibid., p. 96.

12. Harold Kaplan, Benjamin Sadock, Jack Grebb, *Synopsis of Psychiatry*, 7th Ed. (Baltimore: William and Wilkins, 1994), pp. 237–53, 742, 743.

13. Patricia H. Werhane, "Moral Imagination and the Search for Ethical Decision Making and Management," *Business Ethics Quarterly*, Ruffin Series, 1 (n.d.): 81, 82.

14. Ibid., pp. 88–91.

15. Philippa Foot, "Moral Beliefs," in Tom Carson and Paul Moser (eds.), *Morality and the Good Life* (New York: Oxford University Press, 1997), pp. 104–15. (Appears originally in *Proceedings of the Aristotelian Society* 59 [1959]: 83–104.)

4

BUSINESS ETHICS

Philosophy [like ethics] is not a theory but an activity.

—Ludwig Wittgenstein

BUSINESS ETHICS AS APPLIED ETHICS

Taking Ethical Theory and Applying It

Business ethics is a form of applied ethics. There is some disagreement about what applied ethics is. One understanding is that, in applied ethics, we take ethical theory (for example, Kantian duty-based ethics or utilitarianism) and "apply" it directly to concrete circumstances or decisions. For example, you could give a utilitarian analysis of insider trading or a Kantian criticism of executive compensation practices. Much of the early work in the academic business ethics field has this flavor. This way of approaching applied ethics is intellectually respectable, and much can be learned from pursuing it. However, as a practical guide to action it has an important shortcoming: Which ethical theory do you choose?

This is no small concern. There are different ethical theories precisely because there are differing judgments about what ought to be done in some controversial circumstances. Take, for example, insider trading. Ethical theories in which notions of fairness play a prominent role (for example, Kantian duty-based ethics) can be used to condemn insider trading as taking unfair advantage of information not available generally in the market. By contrast, ethical theories in which consequences are the main consideration (for example, utilitarianism) can be used to defend insider trading. That is because the practice efficiently transfers private information to the public market, making stock prices more closely reflect the financial prospects of firms. That, in turn, leads people to make more rational investment decisions and create greater wealth and well-being overall.[1]

So, concluding whether engaging in insider trading is an affront to others or, alternatively, a service to them compels a choice of theories. However, the "Which ethical theory is best?" debate is centuries old and shows no sign of reaching a quick conclusion. Meanwhile, you have to decide what to do now, in the circumstances of the moment. A choice has to be made. Not deciding is the same as making a choice. It's choosing the status quo.

Our point is that treating business ethics as an exercise in applying ethical theory to concrete circumstances isn't often a promising approach. In practice, you want to reach a conclusion and make a decision you can be reasonably confident of. However, a decision depending upon the superiority of one ethical theory over the others is not one you can be confident of. For every proponent of that theory, you can find at least one opponent. Applying ethical theory to concrete circumstances only duplicates the debates and disagreements that characterize ethical theory. What is more, it does this in precisely the controversial and difficult circumstances where it is not clear what ought to be done—the very circumstances in which you need help the most.

Constructing Ethical Theory and Then Applying It

This problem may make a different approach to applied ethics attractive. In this approach, we should develop novel practice- or venue-specific ethical theories and then apply those to concrete circumstances or decisions. For example, you could construct an ethical theory intended to speak particularly to the problems of corporate governance. In business ethics, this approach is popular. Stakeholder theory is a prominent example.[2]

According to stakeholder theory, the firm ought to be governed in the joint interests of all of those who have a substantial relationship with the firm, such as shareholders, employees, suppliers, customers, and the communities in which the firm does business. When stakeholder interests conflict, stakeholder theorists counsel weighing and balancing competing interests; trading one off against another in pursuit of the greatest joint satisfaction of all of them.[3]

This approach is attractive. The problem, however, is that it's *too* attractive. Just like the ethical theories we discussed above, there are differing and sometimes competing practice- or venue-specific ethical theories. For example, some view Tom Donaldson and Tom Dunfee's integrative social contracts theory (ISCT) as a rival to stakeholder theory.[4] A social contract (or contractarian) ethical theory says that the moral norms we are bound by are those that are or would be agreed to by everyone affected. In ISCT, business relationships are governed by a set of actual social contracts, expressly or tacitly agreed to by the participants in the relevant practice. These social contracts establish the moral parameters of the practice, so long as they don't conflict with a hypothetical social contract consisting of what Donaldson and Dunfee call hypernorms—moral rules that have a cross-cultural, and hence, transcendent significance. As you may imagine, because they are differing theories, stakeholder theory and ISCT in some cases can be in conflict.

Consider our earlier example, insider trading. In many countries—the United States, Canada, and most Western European states—insider trading is illegal. In New Zealand, however, insider trading is permitted under the law. One could use ISCT, for example, to justify both its forbidden status in most countries and its permissible status in New Zealand. Stakeholder theory, by contrast, may have a harder time of it. Presumably, the various stakeholders are affected the same way by insider trading whether it goes on in the United States, France, or New Zealand. If it's unfairly harmful to one or more stakeholder groups, then insider trading is morally wrong in New Zealand even if it's not legally wrong. Now, if you're contemplating trading on inside information in New Zealand, ought you to go ahead with a clear conscience, courtesy of ISCT? Or ought you instead refrain because stakeholder theory condemns it as unfair to one or more stakeholder groups? Herein lies the same dilemma that undermined our attempts to apply standard ethical theories such as Kantian duty-based ethics and utilitarianism.

Just as we encountered above, choosing what to do compels a choice of theories. Moreover, as both stakeholder theory and ISCT are reactions to what is sometimes called shareholder theory, your choice is more complex still. As there has been no definitive resolution of the debate among adherents of the competing theories, theory choice is something you can't be confident of. Meanwhile, you have to decide what to do now, in the circumstances of the moment. A choice has to be made. Not deciding is the same as making a choice. It's choosing the status quo.

The first two approaches we discussed have a lot in common. A theory is used or constructed for the purpose of applying it to a concrete circumstance or decision. Multiple theories have been used or constructed. Consequently, in difficult cases—the cases in which we actually need help—the theories split and we are left with the same problem we started with. In both the approaches we discussed, the "applied" in applied ethics refers to what happens to a general theory in a particular situation.

But perhaps "applied" shouldn't refer to a general theory applied in a particular situation. Instead "applied" could refer to something suggested by the great nineteenth-century moral philosopher, John Stuart Mill.

MILL ON SECONDARY MORAL PRINCIPLES

In *Utilitarianism*, Mill argues that there are two levels of moral discourse, not just one. The first or "higher" level of moral discourse is concerned with justification. Justification is explaining the *why* of a moral judgment. For example, utilitarianism tells you that you ought to do something *because* it promotes maximal happiness for everyone involved. Similarly, Kantian duty-based ethics tells you that you ought to do something *because* it respects the essential humanity of yourself and others. By the same token, a social contract–based ethical theory tells you that you ought to do something *because* it is what everyone would have agreed to if the question were put to them beforehand. Justification is everything that comes after the *because*. Mill called these principles of justification *fundamental moral principles*. What we've been calling ethical theory consists mainly of fundamental moral principles.[5]

Mill, of course, was arguing that utilitarianism is the best framework for moral justification. (If not, *Utilitarianism* would be a lousy title for his work.) However, he also argued that we usually shouldn't apply utilitarianism's justification principle—the Principle of Utility—directly to our choices or actions. Instead, Mill says we should guide our conduct by moral rules of thumb. "Whatever we adopt as the fundamental principle of morality, we require subordinate principles to apply it by [. . .]"[5]

What are moral rules of thumb? Generally speaking, they are action guides that we habitually refer to when making decisions. They are an encapsulation of the wisdom accumulated by human beings through experience. Says Mill:

> During all that time mankind have been learning by experience the tendencies of actions; on which experience all prudence, as well as all the morality of life, is dependent.[6]

Think, for example, about promises. Your parents probably taught you, "When you make a promise, you ought to keep it." Notice that this common sense principle tells you *what* to do, not *why* you should do it. It's not a principle of justification. Instead, it's an *action-guiding* principle. It doesn't argue; it just directs. It is a conclusion reached by way of the historical, practical experience of human beings with promise-making and promise-breaking. We call on action-guiding principles like this one so frequently and automatically that we often aren't aware that we're doing it. "Always tell the truth," "take only your fair share," "help people in danger"—the list is practically endless. Other principles we appeal to when deciding what to do are often moral rules of thumb in disguise. When a friend suggests doing something likely to be harmful, perhaps you might reply, "But that would do more harm than good!" This is your way of reminding him to do what makes things better rather than worse. That's another moral rule of thumb we guide our actions by. Mill calls these moral rules of thumb *secondary moral principles*. He argues that they are so important you should guide your behavior by *them*, rather than by the Principle of Utility.

But if that's so, why do we need the Principle of Utility or any principle of justification at all? There is a clear division of labor between action-guiding principles and justification principles. We direct our behavior by action-guiding principles, but we *test* and *verify* the rightness or goodness of the action-guiding principles we adopt by referencing fundamental moral principles. Similarly, we appeal to fundamental moral principles to *discover* the action-guiding principles we should follow in new circumstances for which we have no action-guiding principles—for example, by testing them against the Principle of Utility. In other words, secondary moral principles guide our actions while fundamental moral principles (like the Principle of Utility) justify secondary moral principles. Likewise, John Dewey argued that as we grow up and develop, we guide our actions by the conventional rules of our community and culture. It is only when these rules are doubted or challenged that we seek to justify them by appealing to more general principles. For example, rules of civility, or what we often call manners, are justified, ultimately, in respecting the dignity of others.

APPLIED ETHICS AS SECONDARY MORAL PRINCIPLES

Mill's isn't just a quirky point about utilitarianism. Instead, he identifies a deep fact about moral theory. The first formulation of Kant's Categorical Imperative, for example, says that we ought to act only on those maxims that we could rationally will to be universal law. In other words, the Categorical Imperative is a principle of justification. It justifies action-guiding principles (maxims), not actions themselves. According to Kant, we ought to act by reference to these action-guiding principles (maxims). These action-guiding principles (maxims), in turn, are discovered or validated by reference to the Categorical Imperative. Thus, even for Kant, moral reasoning has a two-level structure.[7] One level is devoted to action-guidance. The other level is devoted to justification.[8] Similarly, a contractarian moral theory says that we ought to govern our actions by norms that would be agreed to by everyone, if the question were put to them. This principle of universal agreement is a principle of justification. It justifies or rejects action-guiding principles. Thus, even for the contractarian, moral reasoning has a two-level structure. One level is devoted to action-guidance. The other level is devoted to justification.

If Mill is correct that moral reasoning has this two-level structure, it raises an intriguing possibility. Most of what we think about as "ethics" or ethical theory occupies the first, justification-focused level. Perhaps *applied* ethics is most fruitfully thought of as what goes on at the second, action-guiding level. That is, applied ethics is about identifying the action-guiding principles that best fit a venue or a practice. If we think of business as a venue or a practice, then business ethics is about identifying the action-guiding principles that best fit the activity of doing business.

This approach embraces the nonideal character of practical decision making. When applied ethics is treated as applying principles of justification to concrete decisions of circumstances, there is a perhaps natural tendency to treat it as an exercise in institutional design rather than practical decision making. Faced with the messy, nonideal alternatives real-world contexts almost always present, applied ethicists almost always focus on creating new institutions that (at least in theory) won't generate messy, nonideal alternatives.

We don't deny that institutional design is important. Institutions ought to be designed or reformed for the better. However, telling people what the ideal institutional design should be is no help when those people have to make decisions within the actual institutions they must deal with. The overall effect of applied-ethics-as-institutional-design is similar to what happened whenever one of the authors, as a teenager, went to his grandmother for help with a problem. His grandmother would listen to the problem and then say, "Well, the thing to do is not get yourself in this situation in the first place!" While true, that observation doesn't offer any *guidance* in the actual circumstance.

Problems are best avoided. But observing that problems are best avoided is exactly no help when you actually have a problem. If you have a problem, then by definition you're beyond the point where the problem can be avoided. If Plan A is to avoid all problems, but you nonetheless have a problem, then what you need is Plan B—a way to solve or at least mitigate the problem. In those circumstances, advice along the lines of "apply Plan A!" isn't helpful; it's an annoying distraction from the problem at hand. By the same token, telling business people that what they need to solve the ethical problems they confront is the ideal legal or political framework that avoids all ethical problems isn't helpful; it's an annoying distraction from the problem at hand.

In our view, the principal work of applied ethics is not designing ideal institutions but helping people make the best decisions they can under their circumstances. It says that context matters and making things better in context is an achievement, not something to be lamented because it falls short of the perfect. Applied ethics done right takes seriously the maxim, "Don't let the perfect be the enemy of the good."

Some will be quick to tar our approach with the brush of situation ethics. Situation ethics is an approach to ethics championed by the Episcopal priest, Joseph Fletcher.[9] The right thing to do is always relative to the situation, and the situation determines the right thing to do. However, our view is not that the situation, or context, *determines* the right thing to do. Our view is only that contexts are real. They *constrain* practical decision making. A decision made without reference to context isn't admirably principled, it's stupidly dangerous.

A Physics Analogy

An analogy to physics may make the point clear. In theoretical physics, important breakthroughs are made with the help of simplifying assumptions. One common simplifying assumption is that all physical motion occurs in a vacuum. In a vacuum, matter encounters no friction. If you assume that matter encounters no friction, the mathematical equations describing its motion become more tractable and easier to express. Predictions based upon those equations will fall short of observed behavior, but they will get close. The difference between the predicted and the observed behavior is attributable to friction.

In applied physics, however, things are different. If you're designing a car engine, for example, friction has to be accounted for. To design it without a way to reduce friction the engine parts will encounter when rubbing against each other—for example, by building lubricants into the design—isn't admirably idealistic, it's stupidly dangerous. The car engine built using theoretical physics overheats and locks up. It falls victim to the friction theoretical physics assumes away. In the same way, ideal moral theory applied without an appreciation of context and its limitations either provides no guidance ("The thing to do is not be in this situation in the first place!") or its guidance is stupidly dangerous. Its guidance falls victim to the context it assumes away.

HOW APPLIED ETHICS MIGHT WORK

Understood as identifying appropriate secondary moral principles, applied ethics is in some ways the opposite of ethical theory. Ethical theory describes the ideal best. Applied ethics describes the non-ideal better. Ethical theory describes the all-things-considered. Applied ethics describes the present-circumstances-considered. Ethical theory is there to satisfy demands for intellectual consistency. Applied ethics is there to satisfy the demands of practical necessity. The best ethical theory is built on dilemmas—situations that highlight and bring into sharp relief the *differences* between rival ethical theories. The best applied ethics is built on discovery of the uncontroversial—action-guiding principles that are *acceptable* to all (or at least a wide variety of) theoretical perspectives.

This understanding of applied ethics is itself an aspirational ideal. No body of applied ethics is likely to achieve it in full. Practical ethics is rarely all-inclusive or all satisfying. It is a process rather than a conclusion. However, it is a worthy aspiration because the aim of applied ethics isn't to show that you're clever but to help in making decisions you can be reasonably confident about. Identifying uncontroversial (or at least, less controversial) action-guiding principles is uninteresting from the standpoint of ethical theory. But, as software engineers say, "That isn't a bug, it's a feature." In other words, that's not a failure, but a benefit. For the balance of the book, we will conceive of applied ethics as the activity of governing your actions by principles informed by the best reasons for the context you're acting in. That idea isn't ours; it's James Rachels's: "Philosophy, like morality itself, is first and last an exercise in reason—the ideas that should come out on top are the ones that have the best reasons on their sides."[10]

THE TWO TOUCHSTONES OF BUSINESS ETHICS

Two Deficient Extremes

It's a commonplace to observe that people say business ethics is an oxymoron. (In fact, it's probably more common for business ethicists to observe it than it is for regular people to actually say it.) Some people say that business ethics is an oxymoron because they have a low opinion of business and the people who do it. The general idea is that business is inherently bad or that it attracts people of bad character likes moths to the flame. Other people say business ethics is an oxymoron even though they themselves are business people! Their idea is different, however. They believe that ethics gets in the way of business. Everyone involved in business is a responsible agent, and everyone ought to look out for himself or herself. If bad things happen to them, it's their own fault. In other words, these people favor business without ethics.

At the other extreme are people who are passionate about business ethics and its importance. They believe that business firms and business people should regard everyone as a locus of moral worth. Business ethics is a matter of business firms and business people bestowing benefits on others. It may involve acts of straightforward philanthropy, like giving to a university scholarship fund or making a big grant to the local opera. It may be providing jobs to people who can't get work or maintaining an unproductive and unprofitable plant for the good of the community surrounding it. This is sometimes called *corporate social responsibility*. It sees business ethics mainly as engaging in acts of corporate *noblesse oblige*. People attracted to this understanding see business ethics mainly in paternalistic terms. It is a matter of the big taking care of the small or the strong taking care of the weak. There can be no doubt that the big taking care of the small has something to do with ethics. What is less clear is that it has anything to do with business. For these activities concern not what one is doing when one is doing business but rather what one does with the money one has—whether or not one has it because one does business. In other words, these people seem to favor ethics without business.

We believe that both these views get something basically right and something else wrong. Those who favor business without ethics understand, correctly, that people who do business are responsible agents. If you're doing business, it is because you are a fully formed, autonomous, and rational agent. If you're not—for example, because you're a child or you're mentally infirm—you have no business doing business. You should instead be in the care of others who transact business on your behalf. Business is an activity of and by fully formed, autonomous, and rational agents.

However, it doesn't follow from this that anything goes. It doesn't follow that if something bad happens to you it's your own fault—because you're a fully formed, autonomous, and rational agent. The participants in a marriage are both fully formed, autonomous, and rational agents. But no one believes that members of a married couple have no moral duties to each other or that marriage is a no-ethics zone. To the contrary, we usually understand that marriage is essentially constituted by moral care and concern. A husband who commits adultery has done a wrong to his wife. No one would say to her, "Well, you're a grown up. If you trusted him it's your own fault." In other words, even fully formed, autonomous, and rational agents have ethical duties to each other and are responsible for their actions in regard to other fully formed, autonomous, and rational agents.

Those who favor ethics without business understand, correctly, that people are loci of moral worth. They understand the marriage example and much else besides. Kantian duty-based ethics, for example, is built on the idea that humanity itself is the source of ethical duty. Utilitarianism is built on the idea that the human capacity to experience happiness and to suffer invests each of us with a duty to do things that promote happiness and avoid suffering as much as possible—not just for ourselves but for everyone affected.

However, from the fact that we are duty-bound in some cases, some of the time, to act paternalistically toward others, it doesn't follow that ethical business practice is constituted by acts of paternal kindness. Acts of paternal kindness are justified when dealing with people who are not fully formed, autonomous, rational agents. Infants and the mentally infirm, for example, are proper objects of our paternal kindness. However, it is not morally required and is indeed often wrong to act paternalistically toward a fully formed, autonomous, rational agent. Treating paternalistically someone who has the capacity for rational deliberation and action is, in the Kantian understanding, a failure to respect that person's essential humanity. For essential humanity consists in the capacity for rational deliberation and action. Paternalism denies or overrides that person's capacity for rational deliberation and action, replacing her judgment with yours. If business is an activity by and between responsible agents, then business ethics can't consist mainly of acts of paternal kindness.

A Golden Mean: Both a Locus of Moral Worth and a Responsible Agent

To do business with another person is to recognize that person as both a locus of moral worth and as a responsible agent. That person is a locus of moral worth because she is a person. If she is doing business, it is because she is a responsible agent. The first, rough rule of business ethics is to treat all with whom you do business as both a locus of moral worth and a responsible agent.

What does it mean, in the context of doing business, to treat another person as a locus of moral worth? It is to recognize that business is itself an activity constituted by ethical norms, and that you owe it to those you do business with to follow those norms. As we discussed in chapter 2, business is constituted essentially by trade. Trade is the activity of acquiring property rights from another person by relinquishing other property to that person, on terms established by bargaining. To engage in trade, you need another person, who has something you value, something of value to that person, and a bargain—an agreement about the terms on which you will relinquish what you have in order to gain what you value.

As obvious as that description is, it is easy to overlook just how morally loaded it is. To engage in trade with another person is to regard that person as the *rightful owner* of the thing you hope to acquire. In other words, it entails respect for the other's authority over the thing. To bargain with that person over the terms of trade is to recognize that the person's rational will must be engaged if that person is to part with what is rightfully hers. If the outcome of bargaining is an agreement on the terms of trade, those terms are *promises* each party makes to the other. Even from this simple description, it is clear that to do business with another person is to recognize and respect that other person as a human being, as a bearer of rights, and as the object of a duty to make good on promises made. To take what is hers without her agreement, or to make a promise without following through on it, is not *only* doing something morally wrong to her—theft or fraud—it is doing something *that is not business* with her. Thus, to do business with another person is to recognize that you have certain duties and the other person has certain rights when doing business with one another.

What does it mean, in the context of doing business, to treat another person as a responsible agent? It is to recognize that you are duty-bound to respect that other person's rights, though not necessarily to act in that other person's interests. This is easy to misunderstand because, in most cases, most of the time, we each have an *interest* in seeing that our *rights* are respected. However, being duty-bound to respect someone's rights is not the same as being duty-bound to pursue that one's interests. For example, consider a business deal between Beier and Sellar. They enter into an agreement for Sellar to deliver one ton of widgets to Beier each month for the next twelve months. In return, Beier must pay Sellar $1,000 for each delivery. Six months into the arrangement, the market price for widgets falls to $700 per ton. Beier has a *right* that Sellar deliver to him a ton of widgets this month. However, Beier's *interests* would be better served if Sellar failed to deliver—because then he could buy a ton of widgets in the open market for less ($700) than he has to pay Sellar ($1,000).

Sellar is duty-bound to respect Beier's right—in this case, to a monthly delivery of widgets as called for in their agreement. Sellar is not duty-bound to act in Beier's interests—in this case, to fail to perform and release Beier from the agreement. Why? Because Beier is a responsible agent. Beier is capable of looking out for his own interests. In the context of a business transaction—a zone of human interaction governed by contractual norms—Beier has the power to make and enter into agreements because he is a fully formed, autonomous, and rational agent. Sellar is not his protector or guardian, but an equal with whom he enters into the arrangement. Sellar is, of course, free to release Beier from the arrangement if he wishes or to negotiate with a Beier a new agreement to supercede the old one. But he is not duty-bound to do either of these things because Beier is a responsible agent.

We maintain that the most basic norm of business ethics is to treat those with whom you do business as *both* loci of moral worth *and* as responsible agents. This idea is difficult. It is not an easy recipe for right action. Although vaguely Kantian, it is not action-guiding in the way that "tell the truth" and "keep your promises" are action-guiding. That's why we call them touchstones. However, we will keep this basic idea in mind in the chapters that follow as we lay out what we think are the action-guiding ethical norms of business activity.

CONCLUSION

Applied ethics approached as the application of ethical theory to concrete problems duplicates all of the pitfalls that have made the quest for the One True Ethical Theory an elusive one. Activity-specific ethical theory (like stakeholder theory, shareholder theory, or ISCT) presents the same basic problem. John Stuart Mill's discussion of the two levels of moral discourse raises the possibility that business ethics is more fruitfully pursued at the level of action-guiding norms rather than norms of justification. A practical business ethics has to avoid preaching ethics without business and business without ethics. The best way to do that is to seek action-guiding norms that see all participants in business as both loci of moral worth and responsible agents. Only then does the essentially ethical character of business practice come through. The next chapter, "Trust and Truth," elucidates the essentially ethical character of the most basic activities—bargaining and negotiation.

NOTES

1. Henry Manne's defense of insider trading has exactly this character. See Henry Manne, "In Defense of Insider Trading," *Harvard Business Review* 44 (November–December 1966): 113–22.

2. Stakeholder theory's proponents have advanced it for purposes far greater than issues of corporate governance. However, it probably makes the most sense as a theory of how and in whose interests a firm's top management ought to manage the firm.

3. See, e.g., William M. Evan and R. Edward Freeman, "A Stakeholder Theory of the Modern Corporation: Kantian Capitalism," in Tom Beauchamp and Norman Bowie (eds.), *Ethical Theory and Business*, 4th edition (Englewood Cliffs, N.J.: Prentice Hall, 1993), p. 82.

4. See, e.g., Tom Donaldson and Tom Dunfee, *Ties That Bind: A Social Contracts Approach to Business* (Boston: Harvard Business Press, 1999).

5. See John Stuart Mill, *Utilitarianism*, in John Stuart Mill and Jeremy Bentham, *Utilitarianism and Other Essays* (New York: Penguin, 1987; *Utilitarianism* originally published 1861), particularly chapter II: "What Utiltarianism Is," pp. 276–98.

6. Ibid., p. 295.

7. See, e.g., Immanuel Kant, *Groundwork of the Metaphysic of Morals*, H. J. Paton, trans. (New York: Harper & Row, 1964; originally published 1785), p. 88. There, Kant distinguishes a *maxim* from a *law*. A maxim is a subjective principle by which an agent acts in his circumstances. A law is an objective principle on the basis of which all rational agents ought to act. The first formulation of the Categorical Imperative calls on agents to adopt only those maxims they could rationally will to be laws.

8. Immanuel Kant, *Foundations of the Metaphysics of Morals*, Lewis White Beck, trans. (Indianapolis: Bobbs-Merrill, 1976), p. 41.

9. See Joseph Fletcher, *Situation Ethics: The New Morality* (Philadelphia: Westminster Press, 1966).

10. Christopher Phillips, *Socrates Café* (New York, W. W. Norton, 2001), pp. 2, 3.

5

TRUST AND TRUTH

When trust is destroyed, societies falter and collapse.

—Sissela Bok

Better Business Bureau investigations are guided by one question: Does the complained-of merchant say what they do and do what they say? If so, the merchant is in the right; if not, there's a problem.

—James Baumhart

TRUST

In business and perhaps in all of life, there are three basic ways to deal with others: courtesy, contracts, and trust. By courtesy, we mean manners or etiquette. Manners are not the same as morals and etiquette is not the same as ethics, but both are socially recognized rules for acceptable other-regarding behavior. Both are sanctioned common forms of behavior that allow for nonthreatening and coordinated human interaction. Manners and etiquette are lubricants of civility and necessary ingredients for living harmoniously with others.

The public performance of prescribed forms of behavior is not about acting, mere ritual, or being a *poseur*. Rather, it is a tacit admission that even if there are no absolute answers in life, we have the ability to "tame the self," and, in so doing, balance our relations with other selves. Although courtesy—manners and etiquette—does not constitute a complete ethical prescription for life, it does offer a means to establish and maintain a level of comfort in our various relationships with others.

Although courtesy plays a part in business and business ethics, the primary bonding elements involved in business transactions are contracts and trust. There is an old cliché in doing business: "Strike a deal, shake hands, and then call in the lawyers and write up the contract." Contracts are a formal legal means by which transactors specify, determine, and delimit the normative relationship that will govern their dealings. Where before they may have only owed each other the duties any human being owes to any other human being, by making a contract they promise each other performances that were not owed before the contract was made. Thus, a contract is like a private constitution operating only among the parties to the contract and addressing only the circumstances and the actions that are the subject of the agreement. Written contracts are documents that record and memorialize the substance of the agreement between the parties. Contracts are the product of promises made by two or more people in which the duty to make good on the promise is secured by the promises made in return. Thus, for example, in a perfectly ordinary commercial contract, Sellar's duty to deliver ten thousand bushels of soybeans is secured by Beier's promise to pay $2 per bushel, and Beier's duty to pay $2 per bushel is secured by Sellar's promise to deliver ten thousand bushels of soybeans.

The world is a big place, and trading partners rarely consist simply of family, friends, and acquaintances. Therefore, trade between strangers (and if the truth be told, sometimes with families, too) requires specific agreements and contracts that are enforceable by law and that promote both parties' confidence that the other party will fulfill their side of the bargain and not behave opportunistically. According to philosopher Erin Ann O'Hara, contracts and contract law help to create confidence that the other parties involved in the contract will perform as promised. All parties know that there are legal remedies available if the contract is not fulfilled or breached and that the breaching party can be held liable for damages caused by not fulfilling the contractual agreement. For O'Hara, the bottom line of contract theory is that it establishes benchmarks of behavior and performance, specifies obligations and costs, depersonalizes the transactional process, and reduces the amount and types of risk each party undertakes in an agreement.[1]

Although individual business transactions can be based on voluntary acts of courtesy or the judicial enforcement of contract law, profitable and long-term business relations require something more. They take root only in a general atmosphere of comfort, confidence, regularity of behavior, and trust. The nineteenth-century social theoretician Emile Durkheim has suggested that trust is a "precontractual element" in any and all social arrangements. Power, dominance, or coercion (like that exercised by political authorities) can be a temporary solution to the problem of social order, but over time, long-term stability requires something more, something that is part of the ingrained fabric of social relations.[2]

Modern scholarship seems to generally agree that trust is a "fundamental ingredient or lubricant, an unavoidable dimension of social interaction."[3] However, what scholars cannot always agree on is an exact or universally applicable definition of trust. In fact, the only thing that they seem to agree on is Warren Buffet's glib, but rather accurate, comment: "Trust is like the air that we breathe. When it's present, nobody fully notices. But when it's absent, everybody notices."[4]

The problem of not always knowing and fully grasping the basic meaning of words and terms that are a regular part of your vocabulary is by no means a new or rare phenomenon. In the *Philosophical Investigations*, Ludwig Wittgenstein pointed out that in both ordinary and professional conversations, we use a large number of words that we do not know or can't actually define. He uses the word *game* as his prime example (or how about a much overused word such as *love?*). His point is that even though we cannot give a complete or single definition to these seemingly simple words, we use them all the time. W. B. Gallie refers to these kinds of words as *essentially contested concepts* and argues that they are a part of our regular lives and vocabulary. Having said all of this, let's at least attempt to come up with a working formula or definition of what we mean by the concept of trust.

Part of the problem of coming up with a working definition of trust is that until relatively recently, we have not fully understood how trust occurs, or how it becomes such a critical part of our social fabric and outlook on life. According to the sociologist James S. Coleman, trust is not a freestanding, self-created, or self-contained phenomenon. Coleman argues that trust comes out of, and is created and shaped by, our network of relationships, as well as the standards and values that are embedded in our given social structure. He argues that trust is a by-product of social capital. By social capital, we mean those shared ideas, morals, values, beliefs, and behaviors that make life easier and add value (capital) to our interactions with other members of our social network. Social capital is not one specific idea, value, belief, or behavior. It is rather a variety of different things that make up the social structure of which we are a part and facilitates social comfort, security, and fluidity. In the broadest and most positive sense, social capital is the sum total of the beliefs, ideas, norms, and values that are the shared currency of our social networks and intellectual milieu.[5]

Where they take root, norms and values such as honesty, commitment-keeping, reliability, truth-telling, dutifulness, and responsibility lead to schemes of cooperation that yield a high degree of mutual benefit. Think, for example, of the ease with which you can extract money from an ATM almost anywhere in the developed world. That system depends upon a high degree of trust among and between you, your bank, other banks, and the intermediaries maintaining the computer and communication networks that make ATM transactions possible. It would be easy for each participant in the system to cheat one or more of the others for short-term gain. Moreover, it would be time-consuming and costly for any of the cheated to use the machinery of the legal system to cover her losses. The more likely result of cheating would be the participants' abandonment of the arrangement and the subsequent collapse of the ATM system. It is only the general trustworthiness of the participants in the ATM system that makes its combination of convenience and profitability possible.

By contrast, where values such as avarice, duplicity, and mendacity take root, cooperative schemes become costly (if they occur at all) and yield much less benefit as participants must expend considerable resources to police the bargain between them. Think, for example, of the uncertainty and precautionary action surrounding a wholesale drug deal. The seller fears being robbed and perhaps killed by his buyer, who could well make off with the drugs and his money. The buyer fears the same thing from the seller. Both fear being taken down by the police. As a result, each tends to hire a lot of muscle for security, lookouts to scout the site of the deal, and informants knowledgeable about the police narcotics squad. Each comes well armed, and tensions are high until the deal is done and buyer, seller, and their respective entourages are clear of the danger. Because there is much to gain through duplicity and much to lose by taking others' representations at face value, trafficking in drugs is a costly undertaking made costlier by its low-trust environment.

According to Coleman, although we are rational agents and help to determine and decide our individual specific fates, it cannot be denied that our choices and actions are shaped and constrained by our social context. Embedded in a social structure, our perspectives on self, the world around us, and others are deeply influenced. The quality of our experiences affects the quality of our choices and general perspectives in life. Social capital is the sum total of our relationships with others. It's about our experiences within a family, a community, or a religious or secular organization. It's about comfort levels and our learned expectations in regard to others. It's about our accumulated feelings of safety and dependability.

Social capital can be understood as an unspoken covenant; an agreement arrived at over time by repetition and reinforced by positive feedback. Social capital reduces the fear and tension of dealing with others. It can contribute to greater cooperation and confidence in our interactions with others. In so doing, social capital reduces the need to be constantly on guard. It establishes and reinforces specific cultural markers and standards for acceptable behavior and conduct. It encourages greater risk taking and more complex, long-term business ventures with individuals we are not intimately familiar with or connected to by family ties. Sharing a common stock of social capital, even strangers can trust one another. Their interaction can be more like going to the ATM and less like doing a drug deal.

Although Coleman argues that trust is a by-product of social capital and not its cause, it can be argued that social capital and trust are involved in a symbiotic relationship. In essence, social capital creates the climate for trust and, in turn, trust reinforces the climate necessary for the maintenance of social capital within a network or group. Cultural analyst Francis Fukuyama sums up the issue when he says:

> social capital is an instantiated informal norm that promotes cooperation between two or more individuals. The norms that constitute social capital can range from a norm of reciprocity between two friends, all the way up to the complex and elaborately articulated doctrines like Christianity or Confucianism. They must be instantiated in an actual human relationship: the norm of reciprocity exists *in potential* in my dealings with all people, but is actualized only in my dealings with *my* friends. By this definition, trust, networks, civil society, and the like which have been associated with social capital are all epiphenomenal, arising as a result of social capital, but not constituting social capital itself.[6]

The philosopher Robert Solomon argues that the success of business and the commercial life of our community is directly dependent on the level of trust inherent in the cultural characteristics of that society. In agreement with Fukuyama, Solomon believes that the essential economic function of trust is to reduce the transaction costs of doing business. Like Fukuyama, he maintains that "trust is the precondition for prosperity." And the high-trust societies have a greater potential for forming successful business partnerships while low-trust societies achieve lesser levels of success and economic prosperity.[7] But for Solomon, from both a sociological and philosophical point of view, trust plays a much more profound role in our lives. Trust is not just about the transactional costs of doing business and the simplification of contracts and bureaucratic rules. For Solomon, "trust also provides the preconditions of civil society, civil not just in the sense of getting along," but in a much stronger, ancient sense of *polity*, an organized and coordinated community.[8] For Solomon, trust is an essential human virtue, and all relationships require trust. Like Aristotle, he maintains that trust is the basis of community. People must be able to trust one another in politics, commerce, and battle, and the alternatives to trust are both Machiavellian and Draconian—fear, control, and power.[9]

Psychologists and management scholars have defined an individual act of trust as "the willingness of a party to be vulnerable to the actions of another party based on the expectation that the other will perform a particular action important to the trustor irrespective of the ability to monitor and control the other party."[10] In a more particular sense, "Trust is confidence in the character and behavior of another in regard to predictability, reliability, dependability, integrity, and regularity."[11] Under the umbrella of social capital, trust within a social network creates the reasonable expectations of civility and predicable behavior. Trust allows us to increase the complexity and richness of our lives. And without trust, our relationships are incoherent and uncoordinated.[12]

Think about it: without trust, how could one be able to negotiate the most pedestrian kinds of both consumer and public interactions? As Solomon has so clearly pointed out:

> We generally trust the products we buy; we thoughtlessly stake our lives on them (cars, pharmaceuticals, packaged foods, airplanes, parachutes, bungee cords). We trust the people who serve us, often without checking their credentials. (Do most of us ever look at our doctors' or dentists' professional degrees? How do you know that the waitress did not spit in your soup or drop your sandwich on the way from the kitchen? How many people double-check the pills dispensed by

their pharmacists? How do we know in an emergency that we haven't hired the Three Stooges as our electricians and plumbers—that is, unless the calamitous results are obvious?) Despite the notorious scams and phonies, our attitude toward most business transactions is one of trust, mixed with a certain amount of prudence. If one really accepted the "caveat emptor" (let the buyer beware), it would be difficult to be a consumer at all.[13]

However, it is critical to keep in mind that trust is both important *and* dangerous. It's important because it allows us to have confidence in others and to be able to depend on others for advice, for help, or for our plumbing.[14] It's dangerous because it allows us to be taken in by "con artists" and others who build a relationship of trust *in order to* betray us.[15] In business, the classic example is Charles Ponzi. An Italian immigrant turned Boston businessman, Ponzi coaxed thousands of people into sinking millions of dollars into a complex investment plan involving international postage rates. He claimed that investors would earn a 50 percent return in ninety days. The trick of Mr. Ponzi's plan is relatively simple. The swindler earns the trust of his earlier clients by paying them big dividends with money taken in from later investors. The fact that people seem to be making big profits on their original investments encourages them to continue to invest more money and, in the process, tell others to do so as well. As long as a large group of investors do not cash out and assuming a continuous and growing stream of new investors, mathematically there is no end to the scheme. For Ponzi, however, the scheme lasted only nine months, spanning 1919 to 1920. To this day, the swindle bears his name.

Of course, the contemporary master of the Ponzi scheme would be Bernard L. Madoff. Using a vast network of wealthy friends, family, and business acquaintances, Madoff created an impressive list of investors, who, in turn, spread the word to their friends and associates, creating the air of exclusivity that comes from an "invitation only" policy. Madoff promised annual returns of 10 to 12 percent every year, regardless of market conditions. As global market conditions worsened in late 2008, Madoff's clients became increasingly paranoid about market stability, even though up until that point Madoff had continued to deliver on his promised return on investment. Nevertheless, a number of investors went to Madoff to claim some or all of their investments. At one point, investors were requesting a total of over $7 billion, which Madoff did not have. In December 2008, Madoff was arrested in his $5 million Upper East Side Manhattan apartment for masterminding a $50 to $65 billion Ponzi scheme, which authorities believe began sometime in the 1970s.

Although much of the popular literature refers to trust as a lubricant, a glue, a medium, or an atmosphere, we believe that these metaphors are not accurate. Trust is not an entity, a thing, or a one-time epoxy. Neither static nor inert, trust is a living relationship that we must continue to cultivate through conversations, commitments, and action.[16] Trust is an active part of our lives. Trust is an option and something that we have to reinforce to maintain. Trust is something that we "individually do; it is something that we make, we create, we build, we maintain, we sustain with our promises, our commitments, our emotions, and our sense of . . . integrity."[17]

Trust, like love, doesn't just happen to us; it is a choice. We don't just fall in love. We learn and, ultimately, choose to love. So, too, we learn and choose to trust. Trust is neither a birthright nor a gift that will last forever. Nor can it be taken for granted. Like love, trust dies if it is not cared for and renewed. When a business associate or a friend lies to us, fails to honor a commitment, demeans or belittles us, we begin to doubt the quality of the relationship. If they persist in this sort of behavior, sooner or later the relationship will change. "I can't live or work with her anymore, because I no longer trust her!"[18]

Trusting is a decision that opens the world to us, builds and deepens our relationship with others, and creates new possibilities for us. Trusting involves an enhanced sensibility that allows us to work and coordinate our actions with other people precisely because we are confident of what we are doing.[19] Without trust, neither civility, conviviality, commerce, nor morality and ethics are possible.

TRUTH

The basic building block of trust is telling the *truth*. Indeed, it would be impossible to characterize as trustworthy a person who cannot be counted on to tell the truth. Though it is often cynically denied, truth-telling is the cornerstone of the business transaction. That is because a contract is an exchange of promises. Promises are representations of one's future actions. To promise is to truthfully represent your intended future actions. To falsely represent your intended future actions isn't to make a different kind of promise. It is simply to lie. Integrity is having the fortitude to follow through on your promises, even when it is difficult or unprofitable to do it.

Although truth-telling is implied in the fundamental act of business (contracting, the exchange of promises), there can be little doubt that the temptation to lie is great in business. That is because momentary advantage can frequently be secured by misleading others. Whether it is telling a potential customer that your product does what it doesn't do or convincing a co-worker to cover for you on a hectic Friday by telling him that it will be a quiet day, it is easy to convince yourself that lying is for the greater good when it means meeting a quarterly sales quota or securing a rare three-day weekend. However, as the earlier section on trust indicates, lying can have unintended negative consequences that are much harder to repair than they are to inflict. Whether it is a bad reputation in your industry as a shoddy salesman or a bad reputation around the office, trust abused is rarely trust recouped.

Important though truth-telling is in business, it is important to remember that there are some circumstances in which you are not duty-bound to reveal the truth. Take, for example, a customer who asks you to reveal your company's trade secrets. Here, you are not only not duty-bound to tell the truth but also you are duty-bound to your company not to reveal your trade secrets. But note that this situation would not underwrite *lying* to your customer, for you can maintain your company's trade secrets by merely refusing to answer the question. You can indicate that the customer is asking for trade secrets that you are duty-bound not to reveal. To lie to your customer—by, for example, "revealing" false information—is to protect your company's trade secrets (which is good) but also to lie to your customer (which is wrong).

TRUTH-TELLING IN SETTLEMENT PREFERENCES

This observation raises an interesting question about what is perhaps the most fundamental commercial activity, bargaining over prices and quantities. For that kind of bargaining is attended routinely by a great deal of active deception about the bargainers' settlement preferences or reservation prices. (A buyer's reservation price is the highest price at which a buyer counts himself better off buying than not. A seller's reservation price is the lowest price at which a seller counts herself better off selling than not.) The circumstances are perfectly ordinary—Sellar has a used car; Beier is interested in purchasing it. Sellar is willing to accept as little as $12,000 for the car, but she says she can't take a dollar under $15,000 for it. Beier is willing to pay as much as $16,000 for the car, but he says that his wife won't let him pay anything over $13,000 for it. That is, both Beier and Sellar are not telling each other the truth about their reservation prices. If each told the truth, they would each recognize that there is a range of prices (anywhere between $12,000 and $16,000) at any one of which both are better off transacting with each other. So, wouldn't it be better if they told the truth about their reservation prices?

Suppose that both Beier and Sellar tell the truth about their reservation prices. Each would recognize immediately that, at any agreed-upon price between $12,000 and $16,000, they are each better off transacting with each other than not transacting. That presents two problems. First, there are many prices at which they could transact in a mutually beneficial way. This is a problem because some prices are more advantageous to Beier, other prices are more advantageous to Sellar, and no price is mutually better for both than any other price. In other words, there are multiple solutions to their bargaining problem, but no way to choose one over all the others.

Each recognizing that for any proposed price there is another price that would make him or her better off, they may find it difficult to choose one price to settle on. Lest we think this is an imaginary problem, the game theorist and Harvard Business School negotiation professor Howard Raiffa reports that it is not.[20] In negotiation experiments conducted at the Harvard Business School, Raiffa told each bargainer his or her reservation price and the reservation price of his or her negotiating partner. In other words, each bargainer knew the full contours of the bargaining range. Nonetheless, in many cases, the bargainers couldn't come to an agreed-upon price. Why? Reasons vary. For some it is the competitive urge—the desire to beat the other negotiating partner. For others, it is the thought that the other person *would* pay more (or accept less) and so *should* pay more (or accept less). Whatever the reason, knowing *all* the prices at which they could transact will, in some cases, some of the time, make it harder for people to reach a mutually beneficial transaction.

An idea may have occurred to you. Why not agree to split the difference? If you know my reservation price, I know yours, and all other prices are more advantageous to one or the other of us, why not just meet in the middle and be done with it? Raiffa found that some bargainers in his experiment did just that. But what about the nonexperimental case where Beier and Sellar can't split the difference unless they each reveal truthfully their reservation prices? That gives rise to our second problem. If Beier and Sellar agree to reveal their reservation prices and split the difference, each must decide subsequently whether the reservation price s/he reveals will be truthful or not. Why? Look at it from Beier's point of view. Beier reasons that if Sellar reveals her true reservation price (in this case, $12,000) and Beier reveals his true reservation price (in this case, $16,000), Beier and Sellar will each enjoy half the transactional surplus (in this case, $2,000 each at a sale price of $14,000). But if Sellar is truthful and Beier represents his reservation price to be lower than it is (say, $14,000), then he (Beier) will enjoy more than half of the transactional surplus ($3,000 for Beier, $1,000 for Sellar, at a price of $15,000). Consequently, Beier may be tempted to downplay his reservation price when "revealing" it. However, the same reasoning applies to Sellar. She may be tempted to exaggerate her reservation price (say, $15,000) because if Beier tells the truth she (Sellar) will enjoy more than half the transactional surplus ($3,500 for Sellar, $500 for Beier, at a price of $15,500). Consequently, Sellar may be tempted to exaggerate her reservation price when "revealing it." The real problem emerges when Beier chooses to downplay his reservation price and Sellar chooses to exaggerate hers. In that case, Beier says he will pay no more than $14,000, and Sellar says that she will accept no less than $15,000. That makes it appear to each of them that no bargain is possible—which is bad, because they would each be better off if they *did* bargain anywhere in the *real* bargaining range. Nonetheless, believing that no bargaining range exists, Beier and Sellar do not transact. In other words, adopting the practice of revealing reservation prices and splitting the difference raises the likelihood that people will not transact even when both would be better off if they did. In his experiments, Raiffa observed exaggeration or downplaying behavior among negotiating partners who agreed to reveal their reservation prices and split the difference.

The foregoing indicates that truth-telling may be a hindrance to mutually beneficial transactions where settlement preferences are concerned. Consequently, it may be easy to see how the practice of keeping your reservation price secret emerged. However, anyone who has done a lot of negotiation knows that negotiating parties don't merely keep their reservation prices secret but often actively mislead each other about them as well. Isn't that a case of wrongful lying that should be avoided in business? Our colleague Tom Carson argues that it is not lying because only misstatements *warranted to be true* are lies.[21] (A statement is warranted to be true if, in making it, you are implying that it is true.) According to Carson, statements made about one's settlement preferences aren't warranted to be true. What is more, the other party doesn't need to know your reservation price in order to make a rational decision about whether to transact at any price currently under discussion. Consequently, misstatements about reservation prices aren't lies and don't fail to treat the other party as a locus of moral worth.

In light of Carson's conclusion that misstating one's reservation price is not a lie, at least one of the authors thinks it strange that Carson seeks to justify such misstatements on grounds of self-defense. That is, Carson argues that misstating your reservation price is not wrongful if it is done as a means of defending yourself against similar action on the part of others. If you know or reasonably suspect that your negotiating partner is misstating her reservation price, Carson holds that you are justified in misstating yours. However, a corollary to his view is that it is wrong to misstate your reservation price if you know or reasonably suspect that the other party is not misstating hers. In private discussion, Carson has indicated that if pressed by this person to reveal your reservation price, the most you can do to fend her off is to refuse to answer her queries.

We think this view fails to take account of the social nature of human beings and of the practice of negotiation. Because human beings are sociable, in negotiation we tend to contextualize and explain our proposed prices. In the earlier hypothetical example, Beier says that his wife won't let him pay over $13,000 for the car. Thus, negotiation is less often a dry announcement of offered and counteroffered prices and more like a conversation. That conversation cannot take place when one party to the negotiation is presented with the choice of revealing truthfully his reservation price or saying he refuses to answer your questions. Moreover, we tend not to trust people who say things like "I won't answer that question!" We suspect that it is for the purpose of protecting one's reservation price while maintaining human sociability (as well as the outside possibility that one might get a better deal) that human beings evolved the practice of active reservation price deception. We "reveal" our bogus reservation prices and thereby dare others to take us at our word.

The moral of the story is that reservation price deception makes us better off. It makes us more likely to transact when mutually beneficial agreements are available to us. Although we are not truthful about our settlement preferences, one need not know one's negotiating partner's settlement preferences in order to know whether it is worthwhile to transact at a proposed price.

It is important, however, not to draw the wrong conclusion here. Lying is wrong, and lying in ways that impair the ability of others to make rational decisions is wrong. The Anglo-American common law distinguishes between legally wrongful and legally innocuous deception by appealing to the concept of materiality. At the common law, a misrepresentation is material if it is about the product, its features, or its attributes. Material misrepresentations are wrong because they impair the ability of the potential buyer to make a rational decision about the purchase. For example, it is wrong to tell a potential buyer that the car you have for sale has an eight-cylinder engine when it really has only a six; that it has four-wheel disc brakes when it really has drum brakes in the rear; that it gets thirty miles to the gallon when it only gets ten; and that it has a year left on the warranty when it is really out of warranty. These are lies that deceive and hurt those who take them at face value. Immaterial misrepresentations, by contrast, are representations about things surrounding the product that do not bear on the product, its features, or its attributes. For example, saying that the car is "hip, cool, and cute—the one all the kids want this summer" is classified as puffery—statements that cannot possibly be verified and so no rational person would take them seriously. A seller's reservation price is essentially like puffery. It is a statement of what the seller thinks the car is worth. But the seller has a strong interest in seeing the car sell for as much as possible, so no reasonable person would take this as an objective characterization of the car's value. Because business negotiations are not necessarily zero-sum games—and, absent force, fraud, or mistake are not zero-sum games—the consequences of believing a misrepresentation about settlement preferences aren't harmful. They don't impair the ability to make a rational decision about whether or not to buy at a proposed price. Lying about what you have on offer is obviously wrong, and nothing we have said here could justify it. Lying about what you have on offer undermines the ability of the buyer to make a rational decision in his or her interests.

CONCLUSION

Trust is essential to business. The advantages gained by abusing trust tend to be transitory, while the loss of trust tends to be permanently damaging to your career. Truth-telling is the basic building block of trust. In business, we are duty-bound to tell the truth when doing so would impair the ability of another person to make a rational decision. However, we ought not to reveal the truth where we are duty-bound to maintain confidences (as with trade secrets). Similarly, we may be justified in misrepresenting our settlement preferences in negotiations because people don't need to know our settlement preferences to make a rational decision about whether to transact at a proposed price. Thus, as in other aspects of business ethics, truth-telling is something that must be pursued at the right time, for the right reasons, and in the right measure.

NOTES

1. Erin Ann O'Hara, "Trustworthiness and Conduct," in Paul J. Zak (ed.), *Moral Markets* (Princeton University Press, 2008), pp. 173–203.

2. Adam B. Seligman, *The Problem of Trust* (Princeton, N.J., Princeton University Press, 1997), p. 13.

3. R. C. Mayer, J. H. Davis, and F. D. Schoorman, "An Integrative Model of Organizational Trust," *Academy of Management Review* 20(3) (1995): 709–34.

4. Don Seidman, *How* (Hoboken, N.J.: John Wiley and Sons, 2007), p. 158.

5. James S. Coleman, "Social Capital in the Creation of Human Capital," *American Journal of Sociology*, Vol. 94, Supplement S95-S120.

6. Francis Fukuyama, "Social Capital, Civil Society and Development," *Third World Quarterly* 22(1) (2001): 7–20.

7. Ibid., 5–11.

8. Robert C. Solomon and Fernando Flores, *Building Trust* (New York: Oxford University Press, 2001), p. 11.

9. Ibid., p. 23.

10. Mayer, Davis, Schoorman, "An Integrative Model," p. 71.

11. Al Gini, *Why It's Hard to Be Good* (New York: Routledge, 2006), p. 166.

12. Solomon and Flores, *Building Trust*, p. 9.

13. Ibid., p. 18.

14. Carolyn McLeod, "Trust," The Stanford Encyclopedia of Philosophy. com (Winter 2009 Edition), Edward N. Zalta (ed.) (URL = http://plato. stanford.edu/archives/win2009/entries/trust/).

15. Solomon and Flores, *Building Trust*, p. 34.

16. Ibid., pp. 86, 87.

17. Ibid., p. 5.

18. Ibid., p. 4.

19. Ibid., p. 119.

20. Howard Raiffa, *The Art and Science of Negotiation* (Cambridge, Mass.: Harvard Business School Press, 1982), chapter 4: "Analytical Models and Empirical Results," pp. 44–65.

21. Thomas L. Carson, "Bluffing and Deception in Negotiations," in Robert Kolb (ed.), *Encyclopedia of Business Ethics and Society* (Los Angeles: Sage Publications, 2008), Volume 1, pp. 182–84.

6

COMPETITION

No system of regulation can safely be substituted for the operation of individual liberty as expressed in competition.

—Louis Dembitz Brandeis, Supreme Court Justice

The breakfast of champions is not cereal, it's opposition.

—Nick Seitz, Editor, *Golf Digest*

Competition is the backbone of the entrepreneurial capitalist system. Characterized by the free formation and dissolution of self-directing business firms, entrepreneurial capitalism fosters competition through the overlapping inspirations of entrepreneurs. It may take the form of several automobile companies offering similar models to the same well-defined segment of the car market. Alternatively, it may take the form of the competition between an amusement park and a movie theater for the consumer's entertainment dollar. Where an entrepreneur discovers a genuinely profitable opportunity, competitors are soon to follow.

Competition comes from the Latin *competere*, to seek together, to come together, to join together in an endeavor. Like many concepts in business, competition plays a vital role in our lives. Whether it is the competition to gain admission to an Ivy League school, the adolescent competition between guys to get "the girl" (or girls to get "the guy"), or the competition among pundits to get an op-ed published in the *New York Times*, competition is a defining feature of our social order.

ATHLETIC COMPETITION

The paradigm of competition is probably athletic competition. Upon hearing the word *competition*, it is hard not to think of two football teams facing one another on the gridiron, two tennis players trading ground strokes on the court, or two boxers bobbing, weaving, jabbing, and punching in the ring. Athletic competition is widely understood to be important in character development. It's valuable because of the virtues it cultivates in its participants. In his *Republic* and his *Laws*, Plato argues that the purpose of athletic competition is to teach *completion*, *coordination*, and *cooperation*.[1]

Completion:	The use and testing of one's body
	To extend and expand one's range of physical abilities
	To learn the limits of one's endurance and abilities
	To learn to be comfortable in one's body
Coordination:	To synchronize body and mind
	To anticipate
	To imagine, to visualize
	To plan, to strategize
Cooperation:	Community effort (as in team sports)
	Collective behavior
	Teamwork

Athletic competition diligently pursued is an important avenue to acquiring and becoming habituated to many of the virtues Aristotle identifies. For Aristotle, virtues are the learned habits and actions of a person that contribute directly to the pursuit and attainment of the good life. By forcing a person to confront the fear of defeat, athletic competition inculcates the virtue of *courage*. By encouraging the discipline to maintain and build one's body for play, athletic competition develops the virtue of *temperance*. A competitor who practices the values we refer to collectively as *sportsmanship* becomes habituated to the virtues of *pride, good temper, friendliness, modesty,* and *righteous indignation.* That is because sportsmanship entails being gracious in victory and defeat (pride, good temper, modesty), treating other competitors as adversaries *only* in the context of the game (friendliness), and acknowledging the deserved—and decrying the undeserved—good or bad fortune of oneself and others during competition (righteous indignation). So understood, engaging in athletic competition offers one of the keys to the formation of a good character and a flourishing life. When the British defeated Napoleon at Waterloo on June 18, 1815, their commander, the Duke of Wellington, is quoted as saying, "[t]he Battle of Waterloo was won on the playing fields of Eton."[2]

COMPETITIVE EXCESS

If the Greek sense of competition is not lost entirely in big-time athletics, it is at least obscured. As sports have become big business, completion, coordination, and cooperation have taken a back seat to winning and the financial rewards that accrue to victorious athletes and sports franchises. It is not accidental that from sports' most commercially developed form, the National Football League, we get the famous Vince Lombardi quote, "Winning isn't everything. It's the only thing."

The effect of big-time athletics on our approach to competition can perhaps best be seen by comparing the aftermath of two major college football games separated by almost half a century, each known as "the Fifth Down Game."

Cornell-Dartmouth

On November 16, 1940, undefeated and number two-ranked Cornell brought an eighteen-game winning streak into Hanover, New Hampshire, to face a Dartmouth team with a 3–4 record. Dartmouth held a 3–0 lead until the closing seconds of the game. On the final series, Cornell had a first down and goal to go on the Dartmouth six-yard line. Three plays brought Cornell inside the one-yard line. On fourth down, Cornell was assessed a five-yard penalty for delay of game, and their subsequent fourth down pass attempt fell incomplete. Strangely, the linesman and the referee signaled that fourth down was still to come. On their *second* fourth down, Cornell scored a touchdown as time expired and was declared the winner by a score of 7–3. Both teams filmed the game and, after the error was discovered, Cornell's president, athletic director, and coach agreed that the honorable thing to do was forfeit the game. They did, and a demoralized Cornell lost at Pennsylvania the following week, finishing with a 6–2 record and a disappointing number fifteen in the final poll. In the end, Cornell concluded that winning isn't everything, at least not at any cost.

ESPN football commentator Beano Cook observes that, "Today, if anybody followed [coach] Snavely and [president] Day's honorable lead, especially with the multimillion dollar BCS pot of gold on the line, it's likely they'd be hung—not in effigy, but in person."[3] Although Cook can only speculate what violence people would do if a big-time college football program voluntarily forfeited a game, he doesn't have to speculate about how attitudes toward high-stakes competition and winning have changed the way people in Snavely's or Day's position would respond today.

Colorado-Missouri

On October 6, 1990, Colorado brought a 3-1-1 record into Columbia, Missouri, to face their Big Eight Conference rival, Missouri. In a nip-and-tuck contest, Missouri led 31–27 with about forty seconds to play. Driving the length of the field, a completed pass inside the ten-yard line gave Colorado first down and a goal to go. Playing without timeouts, Colorado ran a hurry-up offense. In the frenetic plays that followed, the official keeping the down marker lost count and became confused. As in the Cornell-Dartmouth game, Colorado failed to score on fourth down but was awarded a *second* fourth down. They scored a touchdown as time expired. Even after the error was pointed out from the press box and video immediately confirmed the error, the referee declared Colorado the winner by a score of 33–31. In the ensuing public controversy, the difference between how Cornell officials responded to their false victory and how Colorado officials responded couldn't be more stark. Colorado coach Bill McCartney evaded questions about the propriety of forfeiting the game, claiming a fifth down was just compensation for having to play on a poorly maintained field.[4] Colorado officials made no effort to forfeit the game and in no way acknowledged that their victory was tainted. Colorado finished the season with an 11-1-1 record and was declared the national champion in the Associated Press postseason poll. Eight years later, at a meeting of the Promise Keepers organization he founded, McCartney expressed his remorse over the way the "fifth down" situation was handled.[5]

VICTORY VERSUS EXCELLENCE

Our lament here is not the pursuit of victory, but the pursuit of victory decoupled from the pursuit of excellence. A victory gained without excellence is like an election "won" by stuffing the ballot box. The point of an election is for the winner to be the *voters'* choice, not the cheater's choice. The winner of such an election is a thug *posing* as the voters' choice. The point of athletic competition is to excel playing *by* the rules, not to *pose* as someone who's excelled playing by the rules.

Another question to consider is: Can victory be pursued without excellence by means other than cheating? The New Jersey Devils' success in the mid-1990s National Hockey League may be a case in point. Exploiting hockey rules governing moving the puck through the neutral zone and encouraging their defensemen to play at the very edge of unlawful tactics like hooking and obstruction, the Devils pioneered a strategy known as the neutral zone trap. The neutral zone trap made for rough, low-scoring, defensive hockey. It neutralized the advantages of teams with superior talent and secured the Devils the 1995 Stanley Cup. Their success spawned imitators, and the NHL suffered a decade of rough, boring, defense-first hockey that saw the league lose both fans and a television contract. Only after a disastrous 2004 to 2005 lockout (unrelated to the Devils' style of play) did the NHL change its rules to promote wide-open play and offensive excellence. The point of the story is not that that the Devils and their imitators were cheaters. Instead, it is that they seem to have pursued victory even to the detriment of playing excellent hockey. They abandoned traditional hockey virtues like deft passing, skillful skating, and swift transitions in favor of a controlled shoving match in which goals were occasionally scored. It was *winning* hockey, at least for the Devils, but it wasn't *good* hockey, and the sport suffered as a result.

A banner example of seeking excellence in play is Brazil's national soccer team, for whom victory is empty unless they play with *panache*. Called the Samba Kings, the five-time World Cup champion Brazilians play a game marked by rhythmic, almost dancelike coordination among their players, featuring spectacular passes and swift counterattacks. If you want to know why soccer is called "the beautiful game," watch Brazil play. Their pursuit of panache comes at a cost, as it leaves the Samba Kings vulnerable defensively. But they would rather lose playing excellent soccer than start reading tennis coach Brad Gilbert's best-selling book, *Winning Ugly*.[6]

SORE LOSERS AND SORE WINNERS

Competitive excess, manifest in an obsession with winning, can be destructive of more than the pursuit of excellence. It can be corrosive of character, as well. We have all experienced the sore loser, whose boorish behavior makes him as unwelcome off the playing field as on it. Ungracious in defeat, he denies the victor well-earned congratulations. Through constant complaint and endless rehashing of his competitive misfortune, the sore loser finds the source of his defeat in everything but himself. He penalizes everyone around him for inadequacies that are, ultimately, his own.

If the sore loser is an irritant, the sore winner is unbearable. Ungracious in victory, she fails to acknowledge the worthiness of her worthy opponent—taunting him instead. She demands that her victory be celebrated and her praises sung long past the point of any proper congratulation, reducing all around her to an adoring entourage. Acknowledging no role for luck or the unpredictable bounce of the ball, she takes her victory as an exact reflection of her worth and importance.

Though they are on opposite sides of the game's outcome, the sore loser and the sore winner share many of the same defects of character. Aristotle's virtues illustrate this.

Pride

The virtue of pride is a mean between the extremes of vanity and excessive humility. Both the sore loser and the sore winner are vain. The sore loser's vanity will not allow him to acknowledge his role in his own defeat. The sore winner's vanity acknowledges no role in her victory but her own.

Friendliness

The virtue of friendliness is a mean between the extremes of unpleasantness and obsequiousness. Both the sore loser and the sore winner are unpleasant. They are in touch with no one's comfort but their own, and they demand obsequiousness from others.

Righteous Indignation

The virtue of righteous indignation is a mean between the extremes of envy and spite. The righteously indignant person is pained by the *undeserved* good or bad fortune of others but pleased by the *deserved* good or bad fortune of others. By contrast, the envious person is pained by the good fortune of others, whether or not deserved. Also in contrast to the righteously indignant person, the spiteful person is pleased by the bad fortune of others, whether or not deserved.

Both the sore loser and the sore winner fail to be righteously indignant, but they fail in different ways. The sore loser is envious. He is pained by the deserved good fortune of his victorious opponent. The sore winner is spiteful. She is pleased by the undeserved bad fortune of her vanquished opponent.

A loss in competition is undeserved if one plays excellently. Think, for example, of the 2009 Wimbledon men's singles final, in which Roger Federer defeated Andy Roddick 5–7, 7–6, 7–6, 3–6, 16–14. In the longest Wimbledon final (in terms of games played) in history, Roddick lost his serve only once—in the final game of the match—while breaking Federer's serve three times. The point is not that Roddick deserved to win or that Federer didn't deserve to win, but rather that Roddick *didn't* deserve to lose. The righteously indignant person is both pleased by Federer's well-deserved victory *and* pained by Roddick's undeserved defeat. It was an epic, excellently played match in which "no one deserved to lose"—an often expressed sentiment in the wake of a close, well-played contest. That sentiment is foreign to both the sore loser and the sore winner.

The sore loser and the sore winner also demonstrate different defects of character. Aristotle's virtues are again illustrative.

Good Temper

The virtue of good temper is a mean between the extremes of irascibility and apathy with respect to one's propensity to anger. The sore loser is irascible. He is angry *just because* he is defeated. He lacks the self-control to keep his anger in check and the ability to keep his defeat in perspective.

Modesty

The virtue of modesty is a mean between the extremes of bashfulness and shamelessness. The sore winner is shameless in her celebration of self. Lacking modesty, she cannot see herself for the overbearing jerk she becomes in victory. She lacks the self-control to keep her exuberance in check and to see her embarrassing behavior through the eyes of others.

SPORTSMANSHIP

Recall that earlier we characterized sportsmanship as practicing the virtues of pride, good temper, friendliness, modesty, and righteous indignation. The sore loser and the sore winner are both *bad sports*, as in the saying, "Don't be a bad sport!" They lack sportsmanship. Their character—both in competition and outside it—suffers as a result.

Viewed against this backdrop, the NFL's rule against excessive celebration of touchdowns and sacks isn't merely proof that the powers that be in *No Fun League* are a bunch of killjoys (as many in the media would have it). Instead, it can be argued that the NFL is trying to develop the character of its players. Most of those players will have to find a career outside of football once their playing days are over. If they are to succeed in the workaday world, their habits and character traits must be *adult* rather than *adolescent*. Less heavy-handedly, the college football coach Lou Holtz used to discourage touchdown celebrations in the end zone by telling his players to "act like you've been there before." Holtz's is a lesson not just for football, but for life.

BUSINESS COMPETITION

Although athletic competition is paradigmatic, is it an apt analogue for business competition? Certainly, we often talk about business as if it is. We refer to business as a *game*. Sales forces are often divided into *teams*, with the purpose of stimulating an athleticlike competition between them. There are prizes for the winners and humbling defeat for the losers. But these superficialities can mislead. Business is competitive, but it's not a game. Indeed, it's not much like a game at all.

Many Winners, Not Zero-Sum

Athletic contests are in an important sense *zero-sum*. What one wins, another loses. Victory in a game has *defeat* as its necessary correlative. In business, however, one firm profiting need not and usually does not have as its correlative the bankruptcy of competitors or the shuttering of their doors. Firms compete, yet many may profit. In other words, competition in a thriving industry is often *positive*-sum.

This point gets obscured by an excessive focus on market share. Take personal computers as an example. Depending upon how you measure it, Apple Inc.'s share of the worldwide personal computer market is somewhere between 5 percent and 12 percent. PCs made by various manufacturers running the Windows operating system make up almost all of the rest.[7] In the ongoing "religious war" between Windows users and Mac users, this is sometimes taken as evidence that Apple is "losing." However, some industry estimates put Apple's share of the personal computer industry's *profits* at around 40 percent. In other words, Apple has found a small but highly profitable segment of the overall PC market.[8] Apple's position is similar in the U.S. market for cell phones. Their iPhone makes up about 8 percent of that market, but by industry estimates Apple reaps about 25 percent of the profits in the handset market. Our point is that business competition is less a matter of someone winning and someone (or many others) losing, but rather of many shades of success. There are many "winners" (firms that survive, prosper, and continue) and many "losers" (firms that go bankrupt and are either reorganized or dissolved). The point of competing in business is to profit, not to destroy one's competition. It can also be argued that these separate winners stimulate competition between each other and the industry itself. Hence, one could look at this as a win-win rather than a win-lose.

Pervasive, Not Narrowly Contextual

Another important dissimilarity between business competition and athletic competition is context. Athletic competition takes place in a *contrived* context. Its relationships aren't intended to cross the boundaries of the playing field. It's not for nothing that ESPN's investigative journalism show devoted to the social impact of sports is called *Outside the Lines*. The Miami Heat's LeBron James and the Los Angeles Lakers' Kobe Bryant are adversaries *on* court. They aren't adversaries off it. Business competition is different. It has no context akin to the playing field. It has no sidelines and no stadium. Many business people are engaged in business competition as much or more outside the office as they are in it. What starts as a relaxing, after-hours scotch on a barstool may turn into a sales pitch or a business presentation if a potential client or customer happens by. Moreover, the effects of business and business competition are far-reaching and unconfined. The Industrial Revolution and the Information Age have transformed our lives for the better, at least materially, in ways our forbears could not imagine. The machinations and duplicity at Enron wreaked financial havoc on the lives of its employees and left a considerable hole in the Houston economy. No athletic event can begin to match business competition for its effect and significance. Although the Super Bowl is arguably the most watched sporting event in the world and generates hundreds of millions of dollars, it is not the game but the *business* activity surrounding it (think Super Bowl ads) that make it a high-economic-impact event.

Ongoing, Not Final

The word *event* points to another dissimilarity. Athletic competition is importantly *final*. The 2010 NCAA men's basketball tournament is *over*. (Duke won.) Men's college basketball will be played again next season, but it will be a *new* competition for a *different* prize. Business competition has nothing like a final buzzer sounding or a chair umpire announcing "game, set, and match to Mr. Federer."

To be sure, there *are* great triumphs and humiliating defeats in business competition, but they are often discovered only with the passing of time. Even then, their significance is often in dispute. Consider again Apple. By many accounts, it conclusively lost the operating system "war" with Microsoft. Asked at a 1997 information technology conference what he would do if he were in charge of Apple, Michael Dell, founder and CEO of Dell, Inc., replied, "What would I do? I'd shut it down and give the money back to the shareholders."[9] Today, Apple's market capitalization far outstrips Dell's. As of this writing in early June 2010, Apple's market capitalization has passed both Google's and Microsoft's, making it the most valuable technology company and the second most valuable overall company.[10]

Our point isn't that Apple is great or that Michael Dell is stupid. Instead, the point is that it's hard to discern the competitive significance of business events. Did Apple lose in its competition with Microsoft? Was Microsoft's victory instead pyrrhic? Had the emergence of the Internet so "changed the game" (to use an overused metaphor in business) by the time victory was declared in the operating system war that its outcome didn't matter anymore? Imagine how unsatisfying athletic competition would be if its outcomes were this unclear. (Look at how angry college football fans are with the less than clear-cut way national champions are crowned in college football's Bowl Championship Series.) In short, business is part of the fabric of life; sporting events are mere episodes.

WAR

As in the case of sports, the language of war is omnipresent in business. If business competition isn't much like athletic competition, neither is it much like battle or war.

Subduing the Adversary

The point of battle is to *subdue* the adversary; to make him *stop* fighting. Battle's object is the *surrender* of the opponent or, failing that, the *destruction* of the opponent. In a war of conquest, the point of the hostilities is to take control of the enemy, his territory, or his possessions. In any case, the aim of war is to *end* the war on favorable terms.

In business competition, by contrast, subduing the adversary isn't the aim. Toyota doesn't make and market their automobiles with the aim of making Nissan stop making cars. Nor does Ford compete with General Motors with the aim of taking control of GM's Buick division. Moreover, market competitors don't compete with the aim of ending the competition. To the contrary, the aim is to profit; to survive and prosper so as to *continue* in competition tomorrow.

Destruction

The essence of war is destruction. We are at war when we aim explicitly to destroy or to overwhelm our adversaries. As in the case of athletic competition, there are many colorful business metaphors drawn from war that we use to motivate ourselves or to convey the urgency of a business objective. Sales professionals may view negotiation as a battle with the customer. Salespeople may take every dollar above their reservation price as a conquest of the customer and her wallet—forgetting that the customer had a reservation price, too, and she may not have paid out all of it to get what she wanted.

Although metaphors of destruction may motivate or communicate urgency, they also mislead about the nature of business, for business is about creating value and sustaining the enterprise. Although there may be destruction, too—the bankrupt competitor, the strategic retreat of a firm from a market segment—that destruction is collateral, not the objective of doing business.

BUSINESS COMPETITION AND
CREATIVE DESTRUCTION

Perhaps the most famous theorist of entrepreneurship, Joseph Schumpeter coined the phrase *creative destruction* to describe the dynamic effects of entrepreneurial competition.[11] In Schumpeter's view, the entrepreneur is an *innovator* bringing new products, new business models, or new business processes to the market. If his innovations are significant they disrupt the status quo, replacing other products, business models, or processes. The entrepreneur's innovative act attracts imitators who make his innovation the new status quo until a subsequent innovation begins the cycle again.

For Schumpeter, the entrepreneurial act is a *creative* act. The entrepreneur creates value that didn't exist before. Due to the forces of competition, this creative act *displaces* the previous product, business model, or process. Sometimes, this displacement involves destruction. More often, however, the displacement consigns a once-mainstream product, business model, or process to a market niche. For example, the mass production of automobiles displaced the horse and buggy as a mainstream form of transportation. Today, horses and buggies still exist, but mainly as a form of amusement or a nostalgic indulgence. Similarly, the emergence of cheap VHS video recorders displaced the technically superior Betamax recording technology, which disappeared from the home video market but continued to be used for professional video applications. Competitors who are slow to adapt to the changes innovation brings may find themselves in bankruptcy—a concrete, destructive effect of innovation and market competition.

We want to argue that competition is not a negative and artificial aspect of business but a natural and positive one. Aristotle argues that any habitual action that produces well-being and leads to the excellent (good) life is a virtue. Competition, the act of being competitive, can be argued to be a virtue, when correctly or properly pursued. In a larger sense, the economic historian Deirdre McCloskey argues that market competition inculcates the virtues that together make up the good and flourishing life. In her article, "Bourgeois Virtue,"[12] McCloskey argues that the pursuit of profit in the market inculcates other-regarding virtues. The need to satisfy the customer promotes the virtue of honesty:

> The honesty of a society of merchants goes beyond what would be strictly self-interested in a society of rats, as in that much-maligned model of the mercantile society, the small midwestern city. A reputation for fair dealing is necessary for a roofer whose trade is limited to a town with a population of fifty thousand. One bad roof and he is

finished in Iowa City, and so he practices virtue with care. By now he would not put on a bad roof even if he could get away with it, and he behaves like a growing child internalizing virtues once forced on him.[13]

For McCloskey, good practice hardens into habit by way of the business person's competitive striving. For so many virtues does this hold true that McCloskey's thesis in "Bourgeois Virtue" has become a multibook project.[14] Making a similar point, the business ethicist Ian Maitland conceives of the market as a *school* of the virtues.[15] Citing an even higher source, the father of economics, Adam Smith, argues in the *Theory of Moral Sentiments* that the human propensity to "truck, barter, and exchange" encourages competitors in the marketplace to be at once self-regarding and other-regarding.[16]

CONCLUSION

Competition is both the fuel of prosperity in market economies and, when confined to its proper place, a source of many of the virtues that together make for a flourishing life. When not confined to its place, it can be the source of vices that define the characters of the sore loser and the sore winner. At its worst, it can uncouple the pursuit of victory from the pursuit of excellence, to the detriment of all. Competition isn't good because it yields a victor. It is good because it yields excellence, good character, and an abundance that allows life to flourish.

Recall that, for Aristotle, a virtue is a mean between two extremes. Virtue ethics seeks balance in all things. A virtuous competitor must find a way to harness the benefits of competition without allowing competition or competitiveness to become her master. She must let competition be her fuel without it becoming the whole engine of her life.

NOTES

1. Al Gini, *The Importance of Being Lazy* (New York: Routledge, 2006), p. 112.

2. Though widely repeated, the quotation is probably apocryphal. See *Chambers 21st Century Dictionary*, online edition (accessed April 26, 2010, at URL: www.chambersharrap.co.uk/chambers/features/chref/chref.py/main?query=PN23642&xref=y&title=biog).

3. Beano Cook, "Beano Cook's Top Ten Moments in College Football," ESPN.com, October 6, 2006 (accessed April 17, 2010, at URL: http://sports.espn.go.com/espn/print?id=2615391&type=story).

4. Dave Kindred, "Where Have You Gone, Ted Williams: Dubious Sports Feats," *Sporting News*, January 6, 1997 (accessed April 17, 2010, at URL: http://findarticles.com/p/articles/mi_m1208/is_n1_v221/ai_19006779/).

5. "McCartney 'Remorseful' about Fifth-down Play," Associated Press, June 20, 1998 (accessed April 17, 2010, at URL: http://sportsillustrated.cnn.com/football/college/news/1998/06/20/mccartney_fifthdown/).

6. Brad Gilbert, *Winning Ugly: Mental Warfare in Tennis* (New York: Fireside, 1994).

7. *Almost* all, because some percentage of personal computers sold run various distributions of Linux and perhaps other exotic operating systems.

8. In personal computers sold at prices $1,000 and up, Apple is estimated to have a market share of 90 percent.

9. Jai Singh, "Dell: Apple Should Close Shop," Cnet News, October 6, 1997 (accessed April 16, 2010, at URL: http://news.cnet.com/Dell-Apple-should-close-shop/2100-1001_3-203937.html).

10. Connie Guglielmo and Dina Bass, "Apple Overtakes Microsoft in Market Capitalization," Bloomberg Businessweek, May 26, 2010 (accessed June 2, 2010, at URL: www.businessweek.com/news/2010-05-26/apple-overtakes-microsoft-in-market-capitalization-update3-.html).

11. Joseph Schumpeter, *Capitalism, Socialism, and Democracy* (New York: HarperCollins, 2008; original ed., 1942), pp. 81–86.

12. D. N. McCloskey, "Bourgeois Virtue," *American Scholar* 63(2) (Spring 1994): 177–91.

13. Ibid., p. 182.

14. See the first in the series, Deirdre McCloskey, *The Bourgeois Virtues: Ethics for an Age of Commerce* (Chicago: University of Chicago Press, 2006).

15. Ian Maitland, "Virtuous Markets: The Market as School of the Virtues," *Business Ethics Quarterly* 7(1) (1997): 17–31.

16. See Adam Smith, *The Theory of Moral Sentiments* (Indianapolis: Liberty Fund, 2009; original publication, 1759). See also Vernon Smith, "The Two Faces of Adam Smith," Distinguished Guest Lecture, *Southern Economic Journal* 65 (1998): 1–19.

7

PARTIALITY AND IMPARTIALITY: LOYALTY AND ITS LIMITS

THE APPEAL OF IMPARTIALITY

The idea that impartiality is central to ethics is a popular one. It comes naturally to ordinary people. The bulk of the intellectual effort among ethical theorists either defends the idea that impartiality is the essence of ethics or seeks to work out the implications of impartiality for ethics.

All of the act-based ethical theories we have discussed embrace the idea. Utilitarianism calls on you to choose the alternative that yields the most net happiness for all affected parties. Everyone's happiness or unhappiness counts. What this means is that what you ought to do is also what anyone else in your situation ought to do. That's just another way of saying that what you ought to do is determined from an *impartial* perspective.

In Kant's duty-based ethics, the duties we have are those that one could rationally will to be universal law. In other words, they are the duties you would choose regardless of your position in the situation.

This idea is captured in the political philosophy of John Rawls (himself a Kantian) by the idea that justice consists of the rules we would adopt behind a *veil of ignorance*—not knowing one's place in the social order for which rules are being adopted.[1] Behind the veil of ignorance, we are *impartial* with respect to the people who will be affected by the proposed duties or rules.

In social contract−based ethics, the principle of universal agreement gives everyone a veto on any ethical norm that will work to his or her disadvantage. Consequently, the ethical rules that can command universal assent are effectively equivalent to those that would be chosen by an *impartial* spectator—someone who has no stake in the bargain and thus no greater sympathy for one bargainer over another.

From this brief sketch, we see the profound influence that the idea of impartiality has had on the development of ethical thought. So profound is this influence that, for many thinkers, ethics *just is* being impartial. But recall our earlier discussion of the two levels of moral discourse introduced by John Stuart Mill. Mill says that one level of moral discourse is populated by fundamental moral principles—justification principles. The other level of moral discourse is populated by secondary moral principles—action-guiding principles. For Mill, we ought to act in accordance with secondary moral principles (action-guiding principles) that are justified by reference to fundamental moral principles (justification principles).

This is important because, as we observed earlier, ethical theories are about generating and defending fundamental moral principles. Applied ethics is about identifying what you ought to do. Whether explicitly or indirectly, utilitarianism, Kant's duty-based ethics, and social contract−based ethics all make impartiality central to the justification for the rules or norms we ought to act by. But the rules or norms we ought to act by don't necessarily call on us to be impartial. Sometimes they do, other times they don't. A couple of examples may make the point clear.

A referee in a basketball game ought to apply the rules impartially to all the players in the game. That is, the referee, as a matter of action-guidance, ought to act impartially when applying the rules.

The referee ought to do this because, from an impartial perspective, the integrity of the game demands it. Thus, reasoning from an impartial perspective, the referee ought to act impartially when applying the rules in a game of basketball.

A mother ought to favor her child's interests over the interests of other children when deciding how to manage her household, spend her time, or dispose of her assets. Put differently, a mother ought to act partially toward the interests of her child as against other children. She ought to do this because, from an impartial perspective, that is one of the constituent duties of motherhood.[2] Thus, reasoning from an impartial perspective, the mother ought to act partially toward the interests of her child.

If the foregoing is correct, it raises an important question: Is ethical business practice like being a referee in a basketball game or like a mother raising a child?

PARTIALITY, IMPARTIALITY, AND BUSINESS ETHICS

The short answer is *both*. There are elements of business practice that are more like being a referee in a basketball game. For those elements, acting impartially is essential to ethical business practice. However, there are also elements of business practice that are more like being a mother raising a child. For those elements, acting partially is essential to ethical business practice.

Whether because of academic training in ethical theory or some other reason, business ethicists have tended to focus on the aspects of business practice that call for acting impartially. That is, they have been quick to identify cases in which wrongdoing consists of acting partially toward the interests of some as against others and right action consists of acting impartially among the affected parties. Take government contracting as an example. Most U.S. government entities are required by law to open government contracts to competitive bidding. Frequently, government entities are required to choose the winner of the competitive bidding process in accordance with a preannounced general rule, such as low-bidder-wins. These rules are motivated both by the desire for efficiency—to be good stewards of public funds—and to maintain integrity in government—because the government is the government for all of us and so shouldn't play favorites among us. Under competitive bidding rules like these, bidders are sometimes tempted to bribe government officials for information about competing bids (so they know the bid they have to beat to get the contract). Some bidders succumb to the temptation and, not surprisingly, some government officials succumb to the temptation to accept the bribes and provide the information. A government official who accepts a bribe and provides information about other bids has acted wrongly. The official has acted partially, in the interests of one of the bidders (by revealing the low bid) when the official is duty-bound to act impartially among all bidders (by keeping the bids secret from all). Whether or not the government official accepts a bribe, to act partially toward the interests of some bidders as against others is wrong. The government official owes it to all bidders and to the citizens to conduct the competitive bidding process in an impartial way. Favoring some bidders over others is a case of acting partially when one is duty-bound to act impartially.

The foregoing is almost surely correct as an analysis of one aspect of the ethics of government contracting. It is also illustrative of cases in which acting partially toward the interests of some as against others is morally wrong. It is a wrong whose antidote is acting impartially toward the interests of all. However, as a form of commercial interaction, government contracting is the exception, not the rule. In all basically capitalist economies in the Americas, Europe, and Asia, the bulk of economic activity is done privately, between private actors. Moreover, although some private firms do some contracting by means of competitive bidding processes, those processes are themselves the exception, not the rule, for private contracting. Consequently, examples such as government contracting are not the ones we want to appeal to in order to illustrate the partial or impartial character of ethical business practice.

Although most business ethicists have been content to merely assert the central role of impartiality in ethical business practice or to focus on cases where it is central, Norman Bowie has tried to justify business ethics' focus on impartiality. In *Business Ethics: A Kantian Perspective*, he writes:

> I maintain that if there is a place for the impartiality requirement in ethics, that place is certainly in the ethics of business relationships. Business transactions are supposed to be arms-length [sic] transactions. According to the prevailing popular morality, the intrusion of personal interests, such as the interests of family and friends, are [sic] inappropriate in most business transactions. To give one's friends or family special consideration in business is often to place oneself in a conflict of interest. It may even put a manager in violation of a fiduciary duty.[3]

Bowie's examples (arm's-length transactions, conflicts of interest, fiduciary duties) and commonsense considerations (e.g., it is frequently wrong to let the interests of family or friends intrude in business transactions) are important ones for discerning the character of ethical business practice. But do they show that the character of ethical business practice is fundamentally impartial?

Arm's-Length Bargaining

Bowie's appeal to arm's-length bargaining is intuitively plausible. Thinking of the typical business transaction, we imagine hardened negotiators bargaining for advantage, each negotiating on behalf of interests that do not include the interests of the other negotiating party. However, two questions arise: (1) What, exactly, has arm's-length bargaining to do with impartiality? (2) Is one generally duty-bound morally to bargain at arm's length before transacting with another person?

What does arm's-length bargaining have to do with impartiality? When bargaining at arm's length, one generally bargains for advantage. That is, one seeks to secure the most favorable terms one can from the other party. Concessions are made not for the sake of the other party's well-being but for fear of losing what is an opportunity for mutually beneficial exchange. One is concerned about the advantage enjoyed by the other party only to the extent that one hopes the other party finds enough advantage in the agreement to make entering into it more advantageous than not entering into it.

By itself, then, arm's-length bargaining appears to have nothing to do with impartiality. That is, it is marked largely by *indifference* to the advantage secured by the other party, not by impartiality toward that other party. However, implied by indifference to the advantage secured by the other party is indifference among potential negotiating partners. Where one seeks the most favorable terms, one is willing to negotiate with any and all comers. At the outset, you have no reason to prefer one potential negotiating partner over another. To that extent, you are impartial among them.

But although one is impartial among potential negotiating partners when bargaining at arm's length, this isn't an example of *moral* impartiality. Philosopher Troy Jollimore writes:

> A person who chooses an accountant on the basis of her friends' recommendations may be entirely impartial between the various candidates (members of the pool of local accountants) with respect to their gender, their age, or where they went to school. Yet if her choice is motivated solely by rational self-interested considerations then it is clear that the impartiality she manifests is in no way a form of *moral* impartiality.[4]

In other words, even if we recognize a connection between arm's-length bargaining and impartiality, it seems unlikely that it is a connection also between arm's-length bargaining and *moral* impartiality. However, there might be a connection if one is generally duty-bound to bargain at arm's length.

Is one generally duty-bound morally to bargain at arm's length? Consider a hypothetical case, Kant Construction Company (KCC):

KCC. Manny Kant is the sole proprietor of Kant Construction Company. Although Kant Construction Company has no need for additional employees to handle its current or foreseeable future projects, Manny hires his unemployed brother, Danny Kant, to the position of office manager—a position created expressly for him. Danny is neither a trained nor an experienced office manager. Nonetheless, Manny gives Danny a package of wages and benefits more generous than those typical of office managers in the industry or region. Were it not for Danny's joblessness, and were it not the fact that Danny is his brother, Manny would not have created an office manager position, let alone one with atypically generous wages and benefits.

Scenarios like the one described in KCC are played out with some frequency in family businesses the world over. Moreover, popular morality generally endorses practices like Manny hiring Danny to a position entirely unavailable to others and doing it for the reasons that Danny is his brother, Danny is in need, and Manny has the resources to help Danny.

Of course, Manny's hiring of Danny would be morally wrongful if, for example, Manny advertised the position widely, conducted what was apparently a competitive interviewing process, and represented to others that he would hire the best candidate. Absent facts like these, however, common moral intuitions are that there is nothing wrong with—and perhaps even something commendable about— Manny hiring Danny. More to the point, this is true despite the fact that Manny does not bargain at arm's length with Danny.

Given the everyday nature of scenarios like the one described in KCC, it seems likely that there is no general moral duty to bargain at arm's length before transacting. If there were, family business would itself be a morally suspect enterprise. So, mere appeal to arm's-length bargaining doesn't show that there is a central place for impartiality in business ethics.

However, cases like KCC must be considered against other cases. Frequently, one *is* under a moral duty to bargain at arm's length. When one *is*, to fail to bargain at arm's length is to do a moral wrong. So, how can it at once be true that (1) there is no *general* moral duty to bargain at arm's length and (2) one is *frequently* under a moral duty to bargain at arm's length? To answer that question, we must consider *why* one is under a moral duty to bargain at arm's length *when* one is under that duty.

When is one under a moral duty to bargain at arm's length? Usually, it is when one bargains not for one's own account but for the account of another. Consider a hypothetical case, Scottish Lighting Company (SLC):

SLC. Davey Hume is a sales agent for Scottish Lighting Company, a joint stock company whose shares are owned by Franky Hutcheson, Tommy Reid, Johnny Millar, and a handful of other university professors in Scotland. Scottish Lighting Company has recently increased prices on its lighting fixtures because of surging demand and uncertain availability of the basic materials used to produce them. After a brawl at his Glasgow pub, The Invisible Hand, publican Adam Smith summons his longtime friend, Davey Hume, seeking to purchase lighting fixtures to replace ones broken in the scuffle. Upon hearing the new prices, Adam appeals to his longtime friendship with Davey and asks to be sold fixtures at the old prices. Although he believes Adam will pay the higher price if pressed, Davey agrees and makes a contract binding Scottish Lighting Company to sell Adam lighting fixtures at the old, prerise prices.

In his capacity as sales agent, Davey Hume fails to bargain at arm's length with his friend, Adam Smith. Consequently, Davey does a moral wrong to his principal, Scottish Lighting Company. In agreeing to act as a sales agent for Scottish Lighting Company, Davey assumed the duty to act *loyally* in the interests of Scottish Lighting Company when making sales on its behalf. When negotiating a sale to Adam, Davey subordinated the interests of Scottish Lighting Company to the interests of his friend. In so doing, he failed in his duty of loyalty to Scottish Lighting Company.

Davey Hume's duty to bargain at arm's length is based on his duty to act loyally for Scottish Lighting Company, a duty that flows from his agency relation to the firm. He is duty-bound to bargain at arm's length not because all potential buyers have a moral right to be treated equally or impartially, but only as a means of securing the most favorable price for his principal, Scottish Lighting Company. If a potential buyer asks, "Why are you morally duty-bound to bargain with me at arm's length?" Davey's best answer is, "Because it is necessary to satisfy my duty, as a sales agent, to bargain in the best interests of my principal." In other words, Davey Hume has a duty to bargain at arm's length because he is duty-bound to be *partial* to his principal. The best way to satisfy that duty of partiality is to bargain with those who would do business with his principal at arm's length. Without his duty to be partial to his principal, Davey Hume would not be duty-bound to bargain at arm's length—just as Manny Kant was not duty-bound to bargain at arm's length with Danny Kant in KCC. Where there is a duty to bargain at arm's length in business practice, it arises most often out of an agency relationship.

Agency relations are pervasive features of business relationships, but agency relations are not the only source of moral duties of partiality in business. Consider also fiduciary duties.[5] Fiduciaries are duty-bound to loyally serve the interests of their beneficiaries when acting in regard to the specific project for which the relationship exists. For example, if a trustee must liquidate a trust's assets in order to pay for the education of the trust's beneficiary, the trustee is duty-bound to bargain at arm's length with all potential purchasers of the assets. As in SLC, that is not because of a moral duty to potential purchasers that he be impartial to them, but merely as a means of satisfying the trustee's duty to be loyal to the interests of the beneficiary in the sale of those assets. Without the fiduciary duty, the trustee would not be duty-bound to bargain at arm's length.

To summarize, there is no general moral duty to bargain at arm's length. When bargaining on one's own account, rather than on the account of another, one is morally free to favor family and friends, to give sweetheart deals to some and not to others, and indeed to go through one's whole life making transactions this way. Where one has the special moral duty to bargain at arm's length, it is usually because one bargains for another's account and is thus morally duty-bound to act loyally (that is, partially) in that other's interests. Bargaining at arm's length is frequently the best means of advancing that other's interests. For that reason, one is duty-bound to bargain at arm's length. Thus, the duty to bargain at arm's length, where it exists, satisfies one's duty of *partiality* to another. Consequently, appealing to arm's-length bargaining does nothing to demonstrate a central role for impartiality in business ethics.

CHAPTER 7

Conflicts of Interest

Conflicts of interest are recurrent, pervasive features of business practice. Consequently, if the wrong in a conflict-of-interest situation is acting partially when one has a duty to act impartially, then there is a central place for impartiality in business ethics.

Some conflicts of interest *are* examples of practicing partiality where impartiality is morally required. Consider, for example, judging an athletic competition. The 2002 Winter Olympics were marred by scandal when it was learned that Russian interests had promised French figure skating judge Marie-Reine Le Gougne a promotion in the International Skating Union hierarchy if she scored the pairs figure skating competition to the benefit of a Russian team. In a close contest, Le Gougne's scoring provided the margin that initially delivered a gold medal to Elena Berezhnaya and Anton Sikharulidze of Russia and a silver medal to Jamie Salé and David Pelletier of Canada. Upon discovery of her conflict of interest, Olympic officials deducted Le Gougne's scores from the final results, yielding a tie and gold medals awarded to both pairs.

Clearly, Le Gougne's conflict of interest was a matter of judging the pairs figure skating competition partially, in the interests of Berezhnaya and Sikharulidze, when she was duty-bound to all skaters, to the International Skating Union, and to the International Olympic Committee to judge impartially. Hers was an impermissible partiality where impartiality was morally required.

Some conflicts of interest are, as in the Olympic figure skating competition example, cases where one is partial when one is duty-bound to be impartial. Conflicts of interest in business, however, are more frequently cases in which one is partial to *some people* where one is duty-bound to be partial to *other people*. That is, they are cases like SLC, above, where Davey Hume affords a sweetheart deal to a friend when he is duty-bound to bargain at arm's length so to loyally secure the best price for his principal. This is unsurprising because agency relations are pervasive features of business practice. By contrast, quasi-judicial roles (like judging skating competitions) are not pervasive features of business practice. This is not to assert that they don't exist in business. We have already discussed one example, government contracting. The important thing to see is that, in business, scenarios like SLC are the general or central cases, and scenarios like government contracting are the special or atypical cases.

In summary, the principle that one ought to avoid conflicts of interest doesn't illustrate a central role for impartiality in business ethics. Although some conflicts of interest are violations of a duty to be impartial, conflicts of interest *in business* typically are cases of being partial to the wrong party.

Fiduciary Duties

Like an agency duty, a fiduciary duty is a duty to act loyally, for the interests of the beneficiary. In other words, if special consideration of a friend or family member violates a fiduciary duty, the wrong committed is that of being partial to some (in Bowie's example, one's friends or family) when one is duty-bound morally to be partial to others (the beneficiary). The antidote to this wrongful partiality is not impartiality, but *rightful* partiality—partiality practiced on behalf of your beneficiary. Thus, the principle that one ought to avoid violating fiduciary duties does not show that there is a central role for impartiality in business ethics.

MORAL PARTIALITY IN BUSINESS PRACTICE

Bowie has things half right. He's right that arm's-length bargaining, conflicts of interest, and fiduciary duties go far in demonstrating the moral character of business relationships. He's not right that these three pervasive features of business practice demonstrate that impartiality plays a central role in ethical business practice. When one is duty-bound to engage in arm's-length bargaining, avoid conflicts of interest, and satisfy fiduciary duties *in business*, it is generally for the sake of loyalty owed to a principal or to the beneficiary of a fiduciary duty. As loyalty is a form of partiality, these everyday considerations go far to show the large role played by partiality in ethical business practice.

Agency relations are pervasive features of business practice. Many business people make their living as sales agents, purchasing agents, marketing agents, talent agents, and sports agents. Though they may have job titles that make no mention of it, many more make their living in business as agents in one capacity or another. Anyone who has the authority through his or her actions to contract on behalf of another person or a firm is an agent of that other person or that firm. Any member of a partnership, clothed with the authority to act on the partnership's behalf, is an agent of the partnership. Thus, for example, an engagement partner at KPMG is an agent for the partnership that is KPMG. In the words of law professor Deborah A. DeMott, the reporter for the American Law Institute's *Restatement (Third) Agency*:

> Agency's intellectual distinctiveness is its focus on relationships in which one person, as a representative for another, has derivative authority and a duty as a fiduciary to account for the use made of the representative position. Agency doctrine is two-fold, governing rights and duties between the principal and the agent as well as legal consequences stemming from the agent's interactions with third parties. Agency relationships are numerous and varied and include employment, lawyer-client relationships, and the agency created by partnership.[6]

An agency relationship is not merely a legal relationship. Through contract-as-promise it is a moral relationship, as well. Consequently, agency is arguably *the* pervasive feature of business practice, and its ethics are undoubtedly among the most important, everyday aspects of business ethics. As agents are bound by a duty of loyalty to their principals and, as loyalty is a form of partiality, it follows that the "ethics of business relationships" consist to a considerable degree in duties of partiality.

THE USE AND ABUSE OF MORAL PARTIALITY

Fiduciary duties suffer a poor reputation among business ethicists, who address them almost always in the context of the shareholder-manager relationship in the large, publicly traded corporation. Indeed, the central attraction of stakeholder theory (which we introduced in chapter 4) to many business ethicists is as a *denial* that shareholders are the proper beneficiaries of a special class of duties. As philosopher Joseph Heath observes, "The concept of a 'fiduciary' relation is inherently contrastive. Being a loyal fiduciary involves showing partiality toward the interests of one group, not an impartial concern for the interests of all."[7]

But even if shareholders in a public corporation are *suspect* beneficiaries of directors' and officers' fiduciary care, the governance of public corporations is not the only, or even necessarily the most important, business context in which fiduciary duties loom large. Fiduciary duties do not merely pervade business practice, they are essential in many contexts to doing business ethically. The most obvious examples are firms providing a fiduciary service. Consider a full-service stock brokerage. Upon taking on a client and taking control of her account, the full-service stock broker is duty-bound morally to trade in the account in loyal pursuit of the client's interests, subject to the law. That means that the stock broker must commit funds in the account to investments that are suitable to the financial objectives, preferences, and personal circumstances of the client[8] and that suitability of investments cannot be subordinated to the goals and objectives of others (e.g., the broker's goal to collect more commissions, the desires of others to see the client's funds invested in "green" projects). It would be morally wrong for the broker to be impartial between his client's interests and those of others when plotting an investment strategy for the client's funds. For that reason, full-service brokers are fiduciaries for their clients.

Similarly, the Employee Retirement Income Security Act of 1974 (ERISA) subjects employee pension funds to standards of fiduciary care in the investment of funds. Thus, a firm administering pension funds for its own employees is duty-bound to make best efforts to enhance the value of the portfolio, even if the best way of doing this is adverse to the interests of the firm and its equity owners; for example, if short-selling the firm's stock is the most promising way of building the value of the portfolio. It would be a moral wrong for the firm to be impartial between the pension fund beneficiaries' interests and other interests that could be advanced through investment of the monies in the pension fund.[9] For that reason, ERISA makes employees the beneficiaries of pension fund managers' fiduciary care.

As a consideration of their pervasiveness in business makes clear, agency relations and fiduciary duties establish the prominent place of moral partiality in business relationships. Ethical business conduct, in the context of these relationships, requires loyal service to one's principal. To the extent that these relationships are pervasive in business, ethical business practice consists in acting partially in the interests of some as against others. Despite this, duties of partiality are largely ignored or treated with suspicion in the business ethics literature. Joseph Heath and Wayne Norman hold that they are ignored because some believe there is no need to stress duties of partiality as business persons find it easy to serve their principals.[10] However, the scandals at Enron, Tyco, WorldCom, Parmalat, and Hollinger are most reasonably read as stories of faithless fiduciaries, not of the overzealous pursuit of shareholder interests.

Some are suspicious that duties of partiality are a license for predation on the beneficiary's behalf. That is, they see loyal service to one's beneficiary as incompatible with moral restraint when dealing with others who are not their beneficiaries. Both of the authors have noticed a tendency among business students to treat fiduciary duties or agency relations as if they *are* a blank check on the mistreatment of others. These students seem to think that, so long as their interests are aligned with those of their principals, then anything done in pursuit of those interests must thereby be "ethical." But this conclusion is clearly mistaken. As human beings, agents have other moral duties besides those that attend agency. As Kenneth Goodpaster observes, the *nemo dat* principle (short for the Latin *nemo dat quod non habet*—"nobody gives what he doesn't have") means that no one can do as an agent what would be morally impermissible for the principal to do himself.[11] In other words, taking on a duty of partiality does not relieve you of your ordinary moral duties that you have to all human beings, all the time.

CONCLUSION

Like ordinary morality, business ethics consists of duties to act impartially and duties to act partially. Each kind of duty arises in different circumstances. However, much more of ethical business practice is composed of duties of partiality than is generally acknowledged or advertised. That is because important, everyday business relationships are constituted by duties of partiality. Agency relations and fiduciary duties are pervasive features of business practice. Duties of partiality do not erase the ordinary moral duties that we have to all people, all the time.

NOTES

1. See John Rawls, *A Theory of Justice* (Cambridge, Mass.: Belknap Press of Harvard University Press, 1971).

2. From a utilitarian perspective, we could reason that child rearing yields the best consequences when it is done by parents for their children in particular. From a Kantian perspective, we could reason that this duty is implicit in undertaking parenthood. From a social contract–based perspective, we could reason that this is what people would agree to be the norm they should adopt.

3. Norman E. Bowie, *Business Ethics: A Kantian Perspective* (Malden, Mass.: Blackwell, 1990), pp. 6–7.

4. Troy Jollimore, "Impartiality," in Edward N. Zalta (ed.), *Stanford Encyclopedia of Philosophy* (Summer 2007 Edition) (URL: http://plato.stanford.edu/archives/sum2007/entries/impartiality/).

5. The word *fiduciary* most commonly connotes a duty to act for another's benefit. It comes from the Latin *fidere*, which means "faithful, dependable," ergo, "duty-bound."

6. Deborah DeMott, "A Revised Prospectus for a Third Restatement of Agency," *U.C. Davis Law Review* 31 (1997–98): 1036–63, 1037.

7. Joseph Heath, "Business Ethics without Stakeholders," *Business Ethics Quarterly* 16(4) (2006): 533–57, 546.

8. John R. Boatright, *Ethics in Finance* (Malden, Mass.: Blackwell, 1999), pp. 76–78.

9. Ibid., p. 118.

10. Joseph Heath and Wayne Norman, "Stakeholder Theory, Corporate Governance, and Public Management," *Journal of Business Ethics* 53 (2004): 247–65.

11. Kenneth E. Goodpaster, "Business Ethics and Stakeholder Analysis," *Business Ethics Quarterly* 1(1) (1991): 53–73.

8

WORK-LIFE BALANCE

We are so close to the world of work that we often can't see what it does to us.

—Bob Black

Every now and then go away and have a little relaxation. To remain constantly at work will diminish your judgment. Go some distance away, because work (and life) will be in perspective and a lack of harmony is more readily seen.

—Leonardo da Vinci

For 95 percent of us, work is an entirely nondiscretionary matter. Most of us must work in order to earn a living. As adults, there is nothing more that preoccupies our lives. From the approximate ages of twenty-one to seventy, we will spend our lives working. We will not sleep as much, spend as much time with our families, eat as much, recreate, or rest as much as we work. Whether we love our work or hate it, succeed in it or fail, achieve fame or infamy through it, like Sisyphus, we are all condemned to push and chase that thing we call our work all of our days. "Even those of us who desperately don't want to work," said Ogden Nash, "must work in order to earn enough money so that they won't have to work anymore!"

Work is not just about earning a livelihood. It's not just about getting paid, about gainful employment. Nor is it only about the use of one's mind and body to accomplish a specific task or project. Work is one of the most significant factors contributing to the formation of one's character. Beyond mere survival, we create ourselves in our work. In his classic article "Work and the Self," Everett C. Hughes argues that work is fundamental to the development of personality. Because work preoccupies our lives and is the central focus of our time and energies, it not only provides us with an income but also a source of identity. Hughes was convinced that even when we are dissatisfied with or dislike the work we do, choice of occupation irrevocably "labels" us.[1] Work is the way we come to know the world and are known to the world. Work becomes our signature on the world.

In the long run, work can prove a boon or a burden, creative or crippling, a means to personal happiness or a prescription for despair. But no matter where we wind up on the spectrum, *where* we work, *how* we work, *what* we do at work, and the general climate and culture of the workplace indelibly marks us and affects what we believe in and hold dear.

Other factors enter into the equation of self-identity; for example, genetic inheritance, race, gender, ethnicity, sexual orientation, religious training, and family background. But even with all of these, work remains an irreducible given, the most common experience of adult life. The lessons we learn at work help formulate who we become and what we value as individuals and as a society. Whatever the conditions of our labor, work shapes us, and unfortunately, sometimes malforms us.

The lessons we learn at the workplace become the metaphors we apply to life and the means by which we digest the world. The meter and measure of work serves as our mapping device to explain and order the geography of life.

Given the centrality of work in our lives—the sheer number of hours we put into the job, the money that we make, the stuff it allows us to acquire, and the kinds of status and success we can achieve on the job—how can work not affect our values and personal ethics?

Work, all work, creates its own self-contained moral universe. Every job, good or bad, creates its own experiences, its own standards, its own pace, and its own self-defined *weltanschauung* (worldview). Every job, depending on the intensity, depth, and duration of the individual worker's involvement, can have either immediate or long-term effects on the worker. The habits we acquire on the job, what we are exposed to, what is demanded of us, and the pressure of peers can change, influence, and/or erode our personal conduct and standards. At the very least: When everybody else in the workplace is doing "it" (whatever "it" is), isn't it natural to at least ask yourself, "Why not me, too?"

Despite the centrality of work in human life, the question "What does the work do to the worker?" is seldom asked.[2] Workers and scholars alike regularly debate the benefits as well as the drawbacks of particular jobs in specific industries, but only rarely do they address the overall impact of work on the psyche, ethics, and character of the worker.

In the last scene of Arthur Miller's *Death of a Salesman*, Willy Loman's family and friends are standing at his graveside, saying their goodbyes, and reflecting on the character and legacy of the deceased. Willy, they suggest, was a dreamer, a schemer, a talker and teller of tall tales, a con man constantly searching for the big score. But for all of his big talk and even bigger dreams, both his mouth and his ideas were too large for his talents and abilities. Willy, they say, was a failure. But even worse, he was the kind of failure who could never admit it, either to himself or to others. And so right up to the end, Willy went on dreaming and scheming and hoping for that one big sale to come along and set him up for life.

Only one of those gathered at Willy's grave defends him. "Nobody . . . blame this man," he says. "You don't understand: Willy was a salesman . . . A salesman has got to dream . . . It comes with the territory."[3] It was Willy's job to smile, talk a lot, glad-hand one and all, says his defender. His job was to sell himself, sell his dream and his ideas, sell his product. It was his job that made him what he was.

The phrase "it comes with the territory," from Miller's play, is now part of the lexicon. It conveys an acceptance of all the parts of a job and of doing whatever you must in order to get the job done. Perhaps Willy Loman was a failure and a fool because he didn't recognize that he had neither the temperament nor the talent for his chosen profession, but being a salesman shaped him; it drew out the best and the worst in him and made him what he was. To paraphrase Winston Churchill, first we choose and shape our work, and then it shapes us—sometimes, forever.

E. F. Schumacher believes that work is part of the "University of Life." Life is a school, a training ground, and in work we become something more than what we are. We need work, we are formed by work, and the quality of our lives intellectually, emotionally, and ethically is directly dependent on the quality of the work we do.[4] Mirroring Schumacher, philosopher Adina Schwartz maintains that mental health requires work. In theory, Schwartz argues, it is at work that people learn skills, practice and perfect a craft, rationally choose actions to suit their goals, take responsibility for their decisions, and learn and grow from observing the consequences of their choices. In framing, adjusting, pursuing, and accomplishing their work tasks, individuals grow in initiative, intelligence, and autonomy. Individuals are then able to translate these learned work skills to other dimensions of their life. For Schwartz there is a direct relationship between the quality of life on the job and off it. The mix of substantive complexity of the job, individual innate intelligence and talent, and the degree of discretion and freedom allowed in work have a direct bearing on who we are and who we will become both as workers and in our private lives.[5] Work is both elemental and formative in our lives, and adults need work for the same reason that children need play—in order to fulfill themselves as persons.

It is important to keep in mind that although we work because we must, it does not follow that work is bad and that all work is punishing, dehumanizing, or degrading. Work can also be satisfying, creative, and pleasurable in the doing. Work can offer us self-expression, recognition, camaraderie, and meaning. According to novelist and radio commentator Garrison Keillor, although our work, our jobs, can be painful and oppressive, they can also be the vehicles for pleasure and opportunity. It is true that robotic jobs are mindless and often the source of misery and woe. However, having a good job, a worthy task to perform, can directly result in a strong sense of self-worth and self-satisfaction. Although "good jobs" are always hard to find, work can be both pleasurable and fulfilling.

Having said all of this, we are convinced that the central problem of our work lives is not so much the work as the overwork. Work can wear us down and wear us out. Work can erase our energy, deplete our resources, and lower our resistance. But worse still, overwork can lead to laxity, mediocrity, and diminished critical thinking.

Our thesis is a simple one. It is easy to allow yourself to work too much. It is easy to lead too hectic a life. It is easy to rest too little. We are tempted to endanger our health by multitasking constantly. Chronic fatigue and exhaustion can lead to a loss of focus, a diminished capacity for careful consideration, and the inability to maintain objectivity and perspective. Even though work gives us our identity, and even if we love our jobs and find creativity, success, and pleasure in our work, we also need to escape from work. No matter what we do to earn a living, we need an antidote to work in order to work well. We need the benefit of leisure, lassitude, and inertia, both for their own sake and to make us more effective as thinkers, as workers, and as human beings.

As a society, we have always lived in a "culture of work."[6] We have always been obsessed with time. Time is money, and we always try to spend it well. We have never been comfortable with the abstract notion of free time. Unstructured time has made us ill at ease. We see time as our most precious commodity. We try to make the most of our time. We fill time, use time, invest and manage time. We strive to be productive at all times. We live by schedules and lists. We consciously manage our work time, much of our play time, and more and more of our family, private time. We have embraced Thomas Edison's dictum that genius is 1 percent inspiration and 99 percent perspiration. We believe that successful people always have time to do something more, and unsuccessful people never have enough time to do what must be done. We are in a constant race with and against time.

Historically, Americans have viewed the active life as morally superior.[7] The tradition of "busy-ness" is part of our moral fabric. We accord kudos to those individuals who make every moment count and whose every movement is regulated by the clock. Traditionally, in this society, we measure meaning by productivity. And now, says James Gleick in *Faster: The Acceleration of Just about Everything,*[8] thanks to the "rapid heart beat of technology" (cell phones, iPhones, Blackberries, texting, computers, Facebook, Twittering), we have seemingly increased the pace and rate of time and change and we are now able to squeeze more and more of everything into an allotted span. We are now manic about speed, says Gleick. The world now seems to operate on five-minute intervals. We are rush freaks. We are time obsessed. "Lose not a minute" is the motto of our age. Multitasking isn't an option; it's a way of life. Hyperactivity is the norm.

Here's the problem. When life becomes an Olympic endurance event ("the Everydayathon"), when the stopwatch is always ticking, when are we supposed to have fun? When will there be time to be a human?[9] As Benjamin Kline Hunnicutt, professor of leisure studies, so aptly put it, "Having to go so fast to keep up, we miss stuff—our existence is truncated. Some things simply cannot be done going full speed: love, sex, conversation, food, family, friends, nature. In the whirl, we are less capable of appreciation, enjoyment, sustained concentration, sorrow, memory."[10]

In a quintessential American way being busy, being overworked, conveys status and self-worth.[11] The busier our schedules, the more important we feel and the more we are able to acquire the possessions and the things that supposedly constitute the good life. In this society, workaholism is considered a clean addiction, and one that is prized by businesses and corporations. After all, what company wouldn't rather have a workaholic instead of an alcoholic employee? Workaholics produce worth, make money, achieve success. Workaholism is one of the only addictions that is not merely condoned but actually rewarded. It is socially accepted and promoted because it is socially productive. We all know people who brag about working sixty, seventy, or even eighty hours a week.[12] Workaholics in effect say: "I know I'm a workaholic, but it's better than a lot of other things I could be! I'm not sailing a yacht. I'm not playing all day long. I'm not taking exotic trips. I'm working my damn ass off!" They assume, as do their families, friends, and colleagues, that they are being dutiful, industrious, and on the fast track to success as it's prescribed in the American Dream.

According to Diane Fassel in her important but underappreciated book, *Working Ourselves to Death*, the American/Protestant work ethic and workaholism are two separate and distinct phenomena. The work ethic is about the role and acceptance of work in our lives. It's about God's calling to work, the dignity and duty of work, the value and purpose of work. It's about personal and communal fulfillment and survival through work. The work ethic is about life and living. Workaholism, says Fassel, is just the opposite. Workaholism is a substitute for life. It's about self-absorbed, compulsive behavior and performance fixation. We have adapted to workaholism, says Fassel, in much the same way a frog can adapt to a pot of boiling water. If you suddenly drop a frog into boiling water it will leap out immediately. But, says Fassel, if you put a frog in a pot of cool water and gradually heat the water to a boiling point, it will remain in the pot until it dies. Fassel contends that this is the perfect metaphor for the state of workaholism in our society today.[13]

The philosopher Josef Pieper said that "we are fettered to the process of work."[14] Translation: We are captives of our jobs; we are consumed and time bound by what we do. Well, you don't have to be a scholar or sage to know, or at least feel, that Pieper is right. Our lives *do* seem busier, fuller, more fatiguing than ever before.

Aristotle once declared that just as the goal of war is peace, so the object of work is leisure. Or, to state it slightly differently, "We are unleisurely in order to achieve leisure." Aristotle believed that work is a necessary but not a sufficient condition for achieving the good life. Work should not be an end in itself but a means by which one is freed to pursue higher interests and goals. For Aristotle, the end, the purpose, the *telos* of life is leisure. We live to have leisure. We do not live to work. Could anything be clearer? Apparently not!

The reality is, because our cultural mythology is so steeped in the hard work and accomplishments of our pioneering forebears, we just don't get it. We just don't do nothing well. We are not known as a nation of relaxers. Despite the 1960s and the Age of Aquarius, we are not a *laid-back* society. We rarely devote ourselves to idleness. Although it sounds like a Zen paradox, we almost never slow down enough to experience the experience of not doing anything at all. We rarely attune our inner ear to the needs of our inner self. We usually stay too busy. We usually do too much, and in the doing, we insulate and isolate ourselves from ourselves and others. We just don't understand the meaning of the concept of leisure.

The *Oxford English Dictionary* defines leisure as "free time," "time which one can spend as one pleases." Leisure comes from the Latin *licere*, which means "to be permitted," suggesting that leisure is about unstructured, free-choice time. For English essayist G. K. Chesterton, leisure "is the noble habit of doing nothing," and what he means by "doing nothing" is to do no practical, utilitarian, or quotidian task. He does not mean that leisure is equal to inertia or to do nothing at all. Rather, leisure is the opportunity to do other than that which is necessary or required; to do as one pleases; to be freed from the mundane; to be free to pursue the unusual, the inexplicable, the irrelevant, the interesting, and the idiosyncratic; to be at leisure is the ability to stop, or to play, or to think, or to decide.

Work is a major part of life, but it should not be the whole of it. As we discussed earlier in chapter 3, we believe that the ethical life is grounded on character. Character, we argued, refers to the enduring marks or etched-in factors that have been impressed on our minds, which include our inborn talents as well as the learned and acquired traits imposed upon us by education and experience. These engravings set us apart, define us, and motivate behavior. One's character determines one's perceptions on the world, one's philosophy of life, what we hold dear, and what we are willing to act for and act on.

Work is a big part of the experience of adult life. What happens to us on the job can and does affect how we see the world, what we value, and the kinds of choices we make. Work can offer us meaning or madness, purpose or pain, but whether its influence is good or bad our work, all work, always has a profound impact on us. No one can be completely neutral about the effects of work on our private and public lives.

As sociologist Robert Jackall has argued in his important book *Moral Mazes*, the pressures of organizational life and the collective personality of the workplace often can conspire to override the desires and aspirations of the individual worker. No matter what a person believes in off the job, says Jackall, on the job we are sometimes required to suspend, bracket, or only selectively manifest our personal convictions. "What is right in the corporation is not what is right in a [person's] home or . . . church. What is right in the corporation is what the guy above you wants from you."[15]

Just as our work boxes us in, delimits our options, and forces moral compromise, so, too, our lack of sufficient rest, leisure, and play enervates us, erodes critical reflection, and impedes our ability to make ethical decisions. Long hours on the job, the frenzy of multitasking, the drudgery of household chores, and the responsibility of children leave too many of us with too little time for leisure, play, and recuperation. We are both an overworked and under-rested society, and rest is a critical component for both physical and psychological well-being. According to the American Family Institute, overwork and the lack of vacation and play time produces immediate and long-term consequences on the individual worker: stress, burnout, lack of focus, increased mistakes, diminished creativity, troubled relationships on and off the job, disruption of sleeping patterns, and health problems.[16]

Play, says psychiatrist Lenore Terr, is not frivolous. It is one of the ways we become human. Play, like laugher, says Terr, is critical at every stage of life. Play, for both children and adults alike, helps us unlock the door to the world and ourselves. Sadly, Terr concludes, the rush of modern life means less spontaneity, more scheduling, and the slow erosion of the time and opportunity to play.[17]

All of us need to play more. All of us need to vacate ourselves from our jobs and the wear and tear of the everydayness of our lives. All of us need to get absorbed in, focused on, something of interest outside of ourselves. All of us need to escape, if only for a while, to retain our perspective on *who we are* and *who we don't want to be*. Vacations, long walks, quiet weekends, down time, alone time, time to think should not be considered a perk or a privilege but rather a necessity of the human condition. We need to not always be doing. Paradoxically, we must studiously do less in order to do more.

Given the pressures of work and the blitzkrieg pace of our lives off the job, too many details get overlooked, too many niceties get lost in the shuffle, and too many standards and values are compromised by the demands of the moment. Here's the problem: When life is lived in the fast lane, when do we have an opportunity to think clearly? When will there be time to be reflective, to be concerned about anything but ourselves? The bottom line seems clear: Fatigue and the frenzy of overstimulation can block objectivity, delimit perspective, and often deaden our ability to calculate and evaluate logically—even and especially about work.

Without true leisure and the chance to rest, dream, and wonder, we are diminished as human beings. And without leisure, rest, and play, we too often simply endure life rather than enjoy it. In Chinese, the pictograph for the word *busy* is composed of two characters, heart and killing.

Newsweek columnist Anna Quindlen is right, "doing nothing is something."[18] For Quindlen we create our public identity in the work we do, but it is in our "downtime" that we create and become our true selves. To paraphrase the words of Josef Pieper, leisure is not only the basis of culture; leisure is the basis of our ethical selves.

NOTES

1. Everett C. Hughes, "Work and the Self," in John H. Rohrer and Muzafer Sherif (eds.), *Social Psychology at the Crossroads* (New York: Harper, 1951), pp. 313–23.

2. E. F. Schumacher, *Good Work* (New York: Harper Colophon Books, 1979), p. 3.

3. Arthur Miller, *Death of a Salesman* (New York: Penguin Books, n.d.), pp. 138–39.

4. Schumacher, *Good Work*, pp. 112–23.

5. Adina Schwartz, "Meaningful Work," in A. R. Gini and T. J. Sullivan (eds.), *It Comes with the Territory* (New York: Random House, 1989), pp. 153–63.

6. Deborah Baldwin, "As Busy as We Wanna Be," *Utne Reader* 61 (January–February 1994): 54.

7. Ibid.

8. James Gleick, *Faster: The Acceleration of Just about Everything* (New York: Pantheon Books, 1999), p. 12.

9. Ibid., p. 277.

10. Benjamin Kline Hunnicut, "A Fast-Paced Look at the Whirl and Flux of Modern Life," *Chicago Tribune* Books (September 19, 1999): 8.

11. Deborah Baldwin, "As Busy as We Want to Be," p. 56.

12. Diane Fassel, *Working Ourselves to Death* (San Francisco: Harper San Francisco, 1990), pp. 28, 29, 30.

13. Ibid., p. 109.

14. Josef Pieper, *Leisure: The Basis of Culture* (New York: New American Library, 1963), p. 50.

15. Robert Jackall, *Moral Mazes* (New York: Oxford Press, 1988), p. 6.

16. Mark Harris, "The Game of Life," *Utne Reader* (March–April 2001): 61, 62.

17. Ibid., p. 58.

18. Anna Quindlen, "Doing Nothing Is Something," *Newsweek* (May 13, 2002): 76.

9

BIG BUSINESS AND THE GLOBAL MARKETPLACE

The business of America is business.

—Calvin Coolidge

Columbus sailed the Niña, *the* Pinta, *and the* Santa Maria *in an effort to discover a shorter, more direct route to India . . . and the magical Spice Islands of the East . . . famed at the time for their gold, pearls, gems, and silk.*

—Thomas L. Friedman

BIG BUSINESS

As we have observed earlier in this book, academic literature and textbooks in business ethics focus almost exclusively on big business. It would be fair to say that the collection of topics discussed is more about the ethics of *bigness* than the ethics of *business*. One manifestation of this near-exclusive focus is the way in which academic business ethicists use the word *corporation* as if it were a synonym for *firm*. We addressed that misapprehension in chapter 2.

Although it is a mistake to treat big business as if it is *all* business, it would be an at least equal mistake to ignore big business in a book about business ethics. Even if big business doesn't dominate the economic landscape the way Hollywood and too many business ethics texts say it does, big business is undoubtedly a real phenomenon. Simply put, big business—large corporations like Microsoft, Big Four accounting firms like PricewaterhouseCoopers, worldwide investment banks like Goldman Sachs—is the consequence of a long, successful, and high-volume history of trade. Brand names known coast-to-coast and around the world—Coca-Cola, McDonalds, etc.— testify to the phenomenal trading success of firms with humble beginnings. Our point is that all big business began as small business.

The usual approach to big businesses taken in business ethics texts is to focus on their institutional character, marvel at their (real or imagined) power, and suggest public policy reforms intended to curb their abuses and moderate their power. A related approach, called corporate social responsibility (CSR), identifies acts of corporate *noblesse oblige* that a socially responsible firm has a duty to perform. Copying these approaches would be easy, but it would fail to address the twin foci of our text, which are (1) to identify the moral virtues that business persons must cultivate in order to do business ethically, and (2) to identify the ethical contours of business activity. To that end, we will address the question of what virtues business people must cultivate to do business ethically when directing the activities of large business enterprises.

In some ways, this is a strange undertaking in a business ethics text. For only the smallest minority of even the most ambitious business people will become C-level executives in large, publicly traded corporations. Those positions are few in number, they are highly prized, and the competition for them is fierce. Perhaps perversely, many of the people who become C-level executives in large, publicly traded corporations do so despite the fact that they didn't intend it. They were executives in small start-ups that grew beyond their wildest imagination—think, for example, of Steve Jobs starting

Apple Computer in his garage, in 1976, with Steve Wozniak and Ron Wayne. Although the likelihood that any of us will become C-level executives is small, it is still worthwhile to consider the moral contours of big business, for it may shed light on the moral contours of doing business generally.

The Consequences of Scale

The defining characteristic of big business is its *scale*. It is *big* business because it is *large* scale. It may be large scale *organizationally*, involving many thousands or even millions of people. Walmart, for example, employs 2.1 million people worldwide.[1] It may be large scale *geographically*, producing or trading in many locations around the world. The wire transfer company Western Union, for example, has offices in at least two hundred countries worldwide.[2] It may be large scale *financially*, generating revenues larger than the gross domestic product of many smaller nations.[3] ExxonMobil, for example, reported 2007 revenues of $358 billion—second only to the worldwide revenues of Walmart.[4] The biggest of big businesses are large scale in all the ways mentioned. What are the consequences of scale for doing business ethically within a big business enterprise?

The first, and perhaps most obvious, consequence of scale is that, through their ethical virtues, those who direct the activities of big businesses have a greater potential to do good. A large firm, whose products are distributed worldwide, has the capacity to change whole societies for the better. A product that is a quantum improvement over its predecessors can change lifestyles for the better and improve our own knowledge and skill. Think of the Google search engine or, for many people, the iPhone. Rare is the small firm that can transform cultures and introduce substantially more attractive lifestyles the way a big firm can. By the same token, through their ethical vices or failings, those who direct the activities of big businesses have a greater potential to do harm. Whereas a roofer who fails once to be diligent in sealing a roof upsets a single household when rain comes, an engineering manager at an automobile manufacturer who fails once to be diligent in approving a brake design may bring injury or death to thousands of people. Conventionally, in business ethics this idea has been pursued under the rubric of stakeholder theory, which we introduced briefly in chapter 4. Originating in the work of R. Edward Freeman,[5] stakeholder theory is widely regarded among academic business ethicists as the most significant idea in their discipline. Stakeholder theory articulates the view that a business firm ought to be managed in a way that achieves a balance among the interests of all who bear a substantial relationship to the firm. Shareholders, employees, customers, suppliers, and the communities in which it does business are the firm's stakeholders. In Freeman's account, the very purpose of the firm is coordination of and joint service to its stakeholders.

This characterization is vague, but deliberately so. For the stakeholder theory literature consists primarily in attempts to address one or more of the questions it leaves unanswered: *Who* counts—that is, who are the stakeholders? *What interests* count? What is *balance*, why is it valuable, and how is someone who directs the activities of a large firm to know what activities achieve it? How are the ends, values, or practices commended by stakeholder theory incompatible with directors and officers extending fiduciary care to shareholders, so that stakeholder theory stands as a rival to the shareholder theory? Whatever the success of stakeholder theorists in answering these questions, there can be little doubt that stakeholder theory's mode of analysis is the one academic business ethicists adopt most readily in considering the moral controversies they address.

Whatever its theoretical basis or merit, we think stakeholder theory is limited by a practical problem. Stakeholder theory best fits a business world in which stakeholder relationships are stable; a world in which a firm's shareholders, employees, customers, suppliers, and the communities in which it does business don't change much over time. The U.S. economy of the 1950s to the 1970s, for example, was one in which you typically worked for the same company from high school graduation until retirement, bought your car from one of the Big Three automobile makers, watched television programs on one of the three major TV networks, and bought your groceries from one of four or five regional grocery chains. In other words, it was a world in which your stakeholder relationships were durable and, at least conceptually, could be the basis of long-term decisions about the future. That world is gone, however. The recovery of the European and Asian industrial economies from the ravages of World War II, technological advances in telecommunications, and the changing tastes of a richer and better-informed citizenry have changed our relationships to business firms in a variety of ways. A dizzying array of automobile choices makes the idea of being a Ford man or a Chevy man quaint. Demand for healthful and organic food has broken the hold Safeway, Kroger, or A&P once had on the American grocery dollar. The average American holds a number of different jobs during her working lifetime. She consumes media from sources so varied (cable TV, satellite TV, YouTube, iTunes, Amazon, Netflix, etc.) that calling the TV networks "major" is more a lazy habit than a description of their place in the modern media environment. The upshot of these observations is that our many relationships with business firms are more transactional and fleeting. Calling them stakeholder relationships and treating them as the basis for long-term decisions focused on durable interests is a nostalgic wish rather than an honest approach to the emerged and evolving economic climate.

Stakeholder theory calls on a firm's management to weigh and balance the competing claims of stakeholders in formulating the firm's strategy. The philosopher Joseph Heath,[6] however, argues that refereeing clashes of competing interests is only a small part of doing business ethically, even in big businesses. An at least equally significant part involves identifying norms of conduct to guide business people confronting *market failures*.

Market Failures

Market failures are circumstances in which the self-interested actions of competing people and firms yield socially counterproductive results. This is usually a result of poorly designed or evolved institutional arrangements. For Heath, business ethics is less about designing a preferred institutional reform and more about business people refraining from exploiting privately beneficial but socially costly market failures. That is, an important part of being an ethical business person is understanding business as an attempt to profit in a way that generates social benefits, rather than trying to profit at the expense of others. Again, think of the canonical market transaction. In it, buyer and seller each part with something each values less in order to gain something that each values more. The buyer parts with a sum of money he values less in order to gain a good or service he values more. The seller parts with a good or service she values less in order to gain a sum of money she values more. Through trade each is made better off than if the trade had not occurred. The transaction is mutually—and hence, socially—beneficial.

Some market transactions and other business activities, however, have effects on third parties. Economists call these effects *externalities*. Some externalities are positive—as, for example, if Bill's next-door neighbor hires a gardener to landscape her yard and Bill derives the benefit of a beautiful view from his living room window. As a third party to his neighbor's transaction with the gardener, Bill enjoys a positive externality. He is better off for the fact that his neighbor transacted with the gardener.

Other externalities are negative—as, for example, if Bill's next-door neighbor hires a deejay to play loud music in her front yard for a party on Wednesday night and Bill is trying to sleep because he has a meeting early the next morning. As a third party to his neighbor's transaction with the deejay, Bill suffers a negative externality. He is worse off for the fact that his neighbor transacted with the deejay.

Some negative externalities are so large that the burdens suffered by third parties exceed the benefits enjoyed by those who initiated the transaction. That is, although the transaction may be beneficial for the buyer and the seller, the benefit is more than offset by the burdens suffered by others. These transactions (or other institutional arrangements) are market failures. Thus, for example, if there are many neighbors who, like Bill, are trying to sleep because they have early days the next morning, the benefits to Bill's next-door neighbor (and her friends) of her transaction with the deejay may be more than offset by the burdens suffered by her sleep-deprived neighbors.

The usual response to well known and recurring market failures is public or private regulation. A city may have a noise ordinance that forbids public performances of loud music. An apartment co-op or condo association may have similar rules built into its ownership agreement. However, not all market failures are well known, and no one may know whether a novel market failure will recur. It is for these unregulated market failures that Heath argues for ethical restraint.

A prominent example of an unregulated market failure was the California electricity crisis of 2000.[7] In the mid-1990s, California's state government sought to reduce retail electric rates for consumers and make electricity provision by public utilities more efficient by creating the California Power Exchange, a short-term marketplace in which regulated public utilities like Pacific Gas and Electric (PG&E) and Southern California Edison would buy, and electricity generators like Enron and Dynegy would sell, electricity. Although billed as "deregulation" by both proponents and detractors, the system deregulated wholesale prices while maintaining caps on retail prices for electricity. Moreover, the utilities were required to sell their gas-fired power plants to private providers. Both buyers and sellers of wholesale electricity were forbidden to enter into long-term contracts. Instead, the utilities were required to meet their wholesale energy needs through short-term purchases on the California Power Exchange. It was not long before power providers learned that they could manipulate wholesale electricity prices by holding electricity off the California Power Exchange market, scheduling transmission of power through the California power grid at inconvenient times, and other maneuvers. These strategies induced rolling blackouts throughout California that left hundreds of thousands of households without power for a number of hours each day. They so raised the gap between the prices the utilities were paying for wholesale electricity and the retail rates they could charge consumers that PG&E

was forced into bankruptcy. The power providers reaped large profits not by providing their customers a valuable service but by exploiting a poorly designed, state-sponsored market.

For Heath, exploiting an unregulated market failure isn't "just business" but instead a predatory act that violates the ethos of business. That ethos involves attempting to profit by making others better off, not worse off. Refraining from such exploitation requires courage, a sense of justice, and understanding that business is an identity-conferring calling rather than just whatever someone does to make money. In short, it requires a constellation of virtues that together form the character of a business person.

GLOBAL MARKETPLACE

Long before the term *globalization*, or *global marketplace*, was coined and gained currency in our collective consciousness, the phenomenon itself—the global market—was already in place. As a term, *globalization* first appeared in a 1983 *Harvard Business Review* article, "The Globalization of Markets" by Theodore Levitt.[8] As a living concept and a basic business fact of life, it has a long and fascinating history—we called it *trading*.

Economically, we no longer are and, arguably, have never really been a series of isolated islands in the stream. Perhaps what makes it feel so different today is the immediacy and near-ubiquity of global trade. As one wag-commentator put it: "No modern consumer is surprised by the fact that the pair of Italian shoes she bought were designed in Milan, engineered in Germany, manufactured in China, exclusively distributed by an American retailer, and all warranty issues are handled by a call-in center in Mumbai."[9] One measure of global trade's contemporary ubiquity is to consider how strange it would have been even forty years ago to advertise to Americans that your product is made in America by Americans—the way computer bag makers Tom Bihn and Waterfield Designs do today. Where once that was the norm for U.S. consumer goods, today it is a point of distinction.

History clearly tells us that international trade has long been a part of civilized human experience. Between the reigns of Hammurabi (2123–2081 BC) and Nebuchadnezzar (605–592 BC), Babylonia became the major player in agriculture and architecture (the Hanging Gardens of Babylon). It was the richest and most prosperous trader in the Fertile Crescent. During Egypt's XVIII dynasty, Amenhotep III (1412–1376 BC) built a fleet of both war and merchant ships that made Egyptian leadership in the ancient southern Mediterranean world absolute. Periclean Athens (495–429 BC) was not just the birthplace of democracy and philosophy, but it was also the site of the great flowering of Greek commerce and the growth of her financial and military hegemony in the Aegean Sea. The Romans, copying all things Greek, laid the foundation of *Pax Romana* on military conquest and an extensive network of roads that facilitated industry and commerce. During the reign of (Caius Julius Caesar Octavian) Augustus (63 BC–AD 14), Rome created an empire that stretched from England to Persia and persisted for four centuries.

When Marco Polo left Venice for the Far East (AD 1269), China was an established player in the trade of silk, tents, and spices. Venice, at the time, was also a powerful city-state. Venetians made a living primarily on the seas, as traders serving Europe, the Byzantine Empire, and the Muslim world. Strategically located on the Adriatic, Venice was by the late thirteenth century the most prosperous city in all of Europe. At the peak of its power and wealth, Venice had 36,000 sailors operating 3,300 ships, dominating Mediterranean commerce and justifying its reputation as the *Repubblica Marinara*.

No account of international trade would be complete without mentioning the most powerful island trading nation of all time— England. The British Empire was built and maintained by its control of the seas, its army, and its aggressive pursuit of trade. At the height of its power Britannia "ruled the waves" and influenced the political and economic geography of most of the known world in the eighteenth, nineteenth, and well into the twentieth century. America, Africa, and Asia were at different times beneficiaries of England's common law tradition and commercial culture, as well as victims of its sometimes draconian colonial policies. Not for nothing was it said that "the sun never sets on the British Empire."

The author of two best-selling books, *The Lexus and the Olive Tree* and *The World Is Flat*,[10] Thomas L. Friedman is arguably today's leading popular chronicler and commentator on "globalization." Friedman employs the metaphorical idea that "the world is flat." Now clearly, says Friedman, the world is not in fact flat. But it isn't round anymore, either! By flat, Friedman means we are now all electronically intertwined and instantly connected. This interconnectivity, Friedman argues, is not limited to business or politics. It also means that individual people can now plug-in, play, compete, connect, and collaborate with more real impact than ever before. For Friedman, technology has changed how we know, what we know, and how quickly we are able to know about ourselves, the world, and the marketplace.[11]

Friedman argues that through personal computers, the Internet, satellites, broadband, telephonic connectivity, texting, Twittering, and Facebook we have created a platform for information, work, and human capital that can be delivered from anywhere to anyone at anytime. For Friedman, "globalization" is a tangible consequence of Moore's Law, which states that the computing power of silicon chips doubles every eighteen to twenty-four months. In the days of the Cold War, the most frequently asked question was: "How big is your missile?" In a flat world the most frequently asked question is: "How fast is your broadband?"[12] If the "world is flat" concept were a brand, its motto might well be the UBS motto: "Our services are now available in 'only' two locations—'Everywhere, and Right next to you.'"[13]

Somewhat modifying Friedman's thesis, we think that there have been three great eras of globalization. Globalization 1.0 lasted from 1492—when Columbus discovered the New World—until 1800. This was an era of brawn and muscle, horsepower, sail power, and, later, steam power. It was an era of competition and colonization where the world shrank from large to medium. Globalization 2.0 lasted roughly from 1800 to 1989. Thanks to the Industrial Revolution, this era was marked by falling transportation costs due to railroads, trucking, and air transport. These were later compounded by falling telecommunication costs due to the telegraph, telephones, and early versions of the Internet. These shrank the world from medium to small.

Globalization 3.0 dates from November 9, 1989, to the present. It shrinks the world from small to smaller due to the liberating power of ubiquitous electronic communication. As Friedman points out, "According to *The Economist*, a three-minute call (in 1996 dollars) between New York and London cost $300 in 1930. Today it is almost free through the internet."[14]

In our 3.0 world, November 9, 1989, is a crucial date from both a metaphorical and a monetary point of view. Monetarily, Friedman argues that "the fall of the Berlin Wall . . . unleashed forces that ultimately liberated all the captive peoples of the Soviet Empire . . . It tipped the balance of power across the world toward those advocating democratic, consensual, free-market-oriented governance, and away from those advocating authoritarian rule with centrally planned economies."[15] The bottom line here seems clear. "The driving idea behind globalization is free-market capitalism—the more you let market forces rule and the more you open your economy up to free trade and competition, the more efficient and flourishing your economy will be."[16] Globalization, the flattening of the earth by means of the ubiquitous telecommunication revolution, means the spread of free-market capitalism to virtually every corner of the world.

Metaphorically, according to Amartya Sen, the Nobel Prize–winning economist, "The Berlin Wall was not only a symbol of keeping people inside East Germany—it was a way of preventing a kind of global view of the future. We could not think globally about the world when the Berlin Wall was there. We could not think about the world as a whole."[17] Of course, the other important date in the early development of Globalization 3.0 that radically reinforces Sen's point is, sadly, September 11, 2001. As half of the world watched, in real time, the terrorist attacks on New York's Twin Towers, we were stunned, shocked, and amazed. As the towers collapsed, many of us, perhaps for the first time, understood at a visceral and not just a cerebral level just how "flat" the world has become and how closely connected we really are.

Globalization, the continuing process of "flattening" and "interconnecting," is not an epiphenomenon or merely a passing trend. It is no longer possible to understand the morning news, to know where to invest your money, or to think in an informed way about the future unless you understand this new system. Globalization is influencing the domestic policies and international relations of virtually every country in the world today. It "is the integration of capital, technology, and information across national borders, in a way that is creating a single global market, and to some degree, a global village."[18]

Famously, former Speaker of the House Tip O'Neill once said, "All politics is local." What he meant is that when push comes to shove, we primarily worry about our own backyards. Politics is the art of the possible in regard to what we need in our own little piece of the world. Only when local needs and wants are met do we even begin to consider other larger needs. At one time business, too, reflected O'Neill's view of the world. The butcher, the baker, and the candlestick maker sought to survive by satisfying the needs of their immediate customers and neighbors. Today, a business situated locally could serve a market anywhere in the world.

The simple reality is that transnational business is no longer the exception to the rule, and the familiar and comfortable ways of talking about business no longer apply. Therefore, the interesting ethical question isn't whether we should globalize or not. History has decided that for us. Instead, the question is what falls out from the fact that we live in a global economy.

Ethics in Transnational Business[19]

Doing business transnationally raises a number of ethical issues that have no analogue in business dealings done within a single country or legal jurisdiction. For example, where ethical norms are in conflict owing to different cultural practices, which ethical norms ought to guide your business conduct in other nations and cultures? Some discussions of international business ethics treat this home-country-versus-host-country question as central. On one hand, adopting host-country norms is a way to respect the host culture and its members. Thus, business people are advised, "When in Rome, do as the Romans do"—as in etiquette, so too in ethics. On the other hand, business people are advised to resist host country norms that are morally repugnant. Therein lies the rub. For example, when bribery of officials is central to doing business where you are, ought you to embrace the practice as a mark of cultural respect or avoid the practice on the grounds that it is morally repugnant?

One common approach to this class of questions is to refer to or to make lists of norms that ought to guide transnational business conduct. Thus, for example, the United Nations' *Universal Declaration of Human Rights* or, more recently, the United Nations Global Compact is suggested as a guide to conduct.[20] The UN Global Compact calls on business firms to:

- support and respect internationally recognized human rights
- avoid complicity in human rights abuses
- uphold freedom of association and collective bargaining
- eliminate forced and compulsory labor
- eliminate child labor
- eliminate all forms of discrimination in employment
- support a precautionary approach to environmental challenges
- promote greater environmental responsibility
- encourage the development of environmentally friendly technologies
- work against corruption in all its forms, including extortion and bribery

Alternatively, whether inspired by something like the UN Global Compact, a preferred moral theory, a preferred theory of justice, or some combination of these, other lists of norms are proposed as guides to the ethical practice of transnational business. Prominent business ethicist Richard De George, for example, advances several guidelines for the conduct of multinational firms doing business in less-developed countries.[21] These guidelines call for:

- avoiding harm
- doing good
- respecting human rights
- respecting the local culture
- cooperating with just governments and institutions
- accepting ethical responsibility for one's actions
- making hazardous plants and technologies safe

The problems with these approaches seem to be threefold. First, they tend to minimize or ignore competitive reality. Imagine that your firm takes seriously the UN Global Compact. You do business in a less-developed country with long-standing environmental and corruption problems. You are implementing a significant environmental initiative in this country but find that your ability to do it depends upon securing licenses from a corrupt government bureaucracy. If you refuse to pay bribes, you will be unable to implement your initiative. Moreover, you will lose market share to competitors who have no compunction about paying such bribes and also lose your economic rationale for locating operations in this country. Ought you to pay bribes in pursuit of environmental improvement or forsake the environment in order to strike a blow against corruption? The UN Global Compact doesn't yield a clear answer. Second, these approaches duplicate the home-country-versus-host-country question they are intended to help answer. Thus, when called on by De George to cooperate with just governments and institutions, which and whose sense of justice ought to guide the determination of whether the governments and institutions are to be cooperated with? Third, even when calling for respecting local cultures and moral norms, these approaches tend to privilege Western conceptions of justice, fairness, and ethics. Thus, in Donaldson and Dunfee's integrative social contracts theory, which we introduced in chapter 4, a *hypothetical social contract*—a concept itself embodying Western notions of procedural fairness—is supposed to settle clashes between home country and host country, including Western and non-Western, norms and practices.

Worse still, the more interesting home-country-versus-host-country cases are those where home-country norms are explicitly extraterritorial and incompatible with host country norms. In "Italian Tax Mores," a case widely republished in business ethics textbooks and anthologies,[22] Arthur Kelly tells of American firms doing business in Italy. American securities regulations, accounting principles, and conceptions of commercial integrity require firms to account for their tax liability (including foreign tax liability) fully and correctly. The reported liability must match what appears on their tax returns. Italian tax authorities, by contrast, take a firm's tax return to be not a full and correct accounting of their tax liability but an initial negotiating position to which the authorities then make a counteroffer. A firm's final tax liability is settled through negotiation between the tax authorities and the firm. Consequently, an American firm's tax liability for its Italian operations will likely never match what is reported on its tax return, in violation of securities regulations, good accounting practice, and conceptions of commercial integrity back home. General principles of good conduct and hypothetical social contracts seem not to speak to what American tax accountants and auditors ought to do, given the institutions and norms that actually confront them in Italy.

Sweatshop Labor

International business ethics has taken on a new urgency with the emergence of globalization. Nowhere has this urgency been felt more acutely than in the debate over so-called sweatshop labor—the hiring of workers in less-developed countries, usually at wages and under work conditions prevailing in those countries, to manufacture products for the developed world.

Opponents of sweatshop labor argue that multinational firms such as Nike wrongfully exploit poor work and wage conditions in less-developed countries. They argue that, when contracting for labor in less-developed countries, multinational firms are duty-bound to pay living wages and ensure that work conditions more closely approximate those that prevail in the developed world.

In a paper much reprinted and anthologized, Ian Maitland[23] argues that sweatshops are for many less-developed countries an important rung on the ladder to economic development. Although small relative to the developed world, wages paid in factories serving multinationals such as Nike exceed, often by a wide margin, those prevailing in the surrounding economy. The same is true of working conditions. Consequently, sweatshops are a force for the better in the less-developed countries in which they appear. They demonstrate the abilities of the local workforce, serve to raise wages as local firms and other multinationals compete for the best employees, and through the extra-market wages they pay they facilitate the personal savings and capital formation on which economic development depends. Demanding that multinationals pay even more so-called living wages—by which is generally meant wages that closely approximate those prevailing in the developed world—is to effectively deny workers in the less-developed world the opportunity to compete in the world labor market. For the outcome of a mandatory living wage is not sweatshop workers being paid more, but multinationals keeping factories in places where the market wage parallels the living wage (usually the developed world). This promises to leave sweatshop workers working for the (lower) prevailing wages and in the (poorer) prevailing conditions that their local economies, without the multinationals, offer. According to Maitland, opponents of sweatshop labor are guilty of allowing the perfect to be the enemy of the good.

Maitland's critics have replied generally by disputing the effects flowing from living wage mandates and other proposals for overcoming sweatshop labor. Denis Arnold and Norman Bowie,[24] for example, argue that Kantian respect for persons demands payment of a living wage. They maintain that the minimum wage research of economists David Card and Alan Krueger[25] demonstrates that raising the wages of low-wage workers lacks the unemployment effect that Maitland predicts. As sweatshop workers earn wages that are usually below those of U.S. minimum wage workers, it is likely that they will escape the unemployment effect.

The complexity of the dispute over sweatshop labor illustrates the complexity of doing business at a distance without intimacy. If we are to overcome the tribalism implied in the Italian phrase *sangue di mia sangue*—the blood of my blood—we recognize very quickly that it is difficult, if not impossible, to advance clear ethical rules for doing business transnationally. Especially when doing business in the less-developed world, it is best to be guided by general principles that should apply when doing business anywhere. The first is the idea that we do business in an attempt to profit while improving the lot of others. That is, we should remember that business is an honorable calling, not merely whatever a person does to make money. One of the first precepts of medical ethics is "first, do no harm." That is an important principle to apply when doing business abroad. Globalization tests the elements of ethics in business. It raises hard questions, worked out at a distance on a world stage. It seems commonsensical that it is more difficult to be unethical in an intimate relationship. Lying to a friend, breaking your word to a co-worker, or cheating on a spouse takes considerable effort and temerity. But at a distance and as the distance grows, our moral compass loses true north and makes mendacity, audacity, and outrageous behavior easier to perform. Just as alcohol reduces our inhibitions, so does distance reduce our ethical acumen. Intimacy is not a necessary condition for ethical conduct, but it makes it easier.

NOTES

1. http://walmartstores.com/Careers/7683.aspx (accessed March 7, 2010).

2. See Hoag Levins, "Marketing Western Union," *Advertising Age* (September 4, 2009) (accessed March 7, 2010, at URL: http://adage.com/video/article?article_id=138817).

3. In the business ethics literature, more is made of this observation than is warranted. It is sometimes claimed that a firm having revenues larger than a given political state shows that the firm "is as powerful" as that political state. This, however, is a non sequitur—a conclusion that doesn't follow from its premises. From the fact that General Motors, for

example, has revenues roughly equal to the GDP of Egypt, for example, it doesn't follow that GM is as powerful as Egypt. Egypt has the power to conscript its citizens for military service, imprison them for criminal activity, and, in extreme cases, to put them to death. GM lacks all these powers.

4. "The Global 2000," *Forbes* (April 2, 2008) (accessed March 7, 2010, at URL: http://www.forbes.com/lists/2008/18/biz_2000global08_The-Global-2000_Sales.html).

5. R. Edward Freeman, *Strategic Management: A Stakeholder Approach* (Boston: Pitman, 1984).

6. Joseph Heath, "Business Ethics without Stakeholders," *Business Ethics Quarterly* 16 (2006): 533–57.

7. See, e.g., James L. Sweeney, *The California Electricity Crisis* (Stanford, Calif.: Hoover Institution Press, 2002); Lisa Royan, "Case Study: The California Power Crisis of 2000–2001" (accessed March 14, 2010, at URL: www.erisk.com/Learning/CaseStudies/CaliforniaPowerCrisis2000.asp).

8. See, e.g., Barnaby J. Feder, "Theodore Levitt, 81, Who Coined the Term 'Globalization,' Is Dead," *New York Times* (July 6, 2006).

9. Al Gini, "Why Get an MBA?," *The Eight Forty-Eight Show*, Chicago Public Radio, WBEZ-FM (91.5), March 26, 2009.

10. Thomas L. Friedman, *The Lexus and the Olive Tree: Understanding Globalization* (New York: Farrar, Straus and Giroux, 1999); *The World Is Flat: A Brief History of the Twenty-first Century* (New York: Farrar, Straus and Giroux, 2005).

11. Friedman, *The World Is Flat*, p. x.

12. Friedman, *The Lexus and the Olive Tree*, chapter 1.

13. Ibid., p. 44.

14. Ibid., Introduction.

15. Ibid., p. 52.

16. Ibid., chapter 1.

17. Friedman, *The World Is Flat*, p. 54.

18. http://www.thomaslfriedman.com/bookshelf/the-lexus-and-the-olive-tree (accessed March 7, 2010).

19. This discussion is taken largely from Alexei M. Marcoux, "Business Ethics," in Edward N. Zalta (ed.), *Stanford Encyclopedia of Philosophy* (Winter 2009 Edition) (URL: http://plato.stanford.edu/archives/win2009/entries/ethics-business/).

20. United Nations, *Universal Declaration of Human Rights* (accessed March 7, 2010, at URL: www.un.org/en/documents/udhr/). United Nations

Global Compact, "Ten Principles" (accessed March 7, 2010, at URL: www. unglobalcompact.org/aboutthegc/thetenprinciples/index.html).

21. Richard De George, *Competing with Integrity in International Business* (New York: Oxford University Press, 1993).

22. See, e.g., Al Gini, *Case Studies in Business Ethics*, 5th Ed. (Upper Saddle River, N.J.: Prentice Hall, 2005), pp. 70–71.

23. Ian Maitland, "The Great Non-Debate over International Sweat-shops," *British Academy of Management Annual Conference Proceedings* (1997): 240–65.

24. Denis Arnold and Norman Bowie, "Sweatshops and Respect for Persons," *Business Ethics Quarterly* 13(2) (2003): 221–42.

25. David Card and Alan B. Krueger, *Myth and Measurement: The New Economics of the Minimum Wage* (Princeton: Princeton University Press, 1995).

10

THE ROLE OF
LEADERSHIP

A fish rots from the head.

—Russian Proverb

Nothing great ever happens until leadership shows up.

—Mike Singletary

We are convinced that whether you are talking about personal ethics or business ethics; whether you're talking about truth and trust in a company; the limits and appropriate use of competition, loyalty, integrity; and how organizations are maintained; it all comes down to leadership. Intentions aside, even the best formulated plans cannot be sustained and actually don't see the light of day (a real action plan) unless and until one's focus is established through effective leadership. Leadership may not be the only answer, but it is the key to any kind of organizational development. Effective leadership doesn't guarantee success, but it gives us hope of it. Ask yourself: What is an organization without leadership? Answer: It's not an organization at all.[1]

Leadership gives form and function to human association, and there seems to be something magical about that. Like moths to a flame, we are drawn to both the successful exploits and front-page failures of individual leaders. We love them, we hate them. We desire them, we despise them. We shun them, and yet we seek them out. Bottom line, we are fascinated by them. Somehow, many of us think that leadership is a magical elixir, and if we can just get the right person, the right leader, in the right job—success will naturally and necessarily follow.

We are in awe of many of our leaders, and we accord them "movie star" status. They become celebrities, icons, secular saints, and cultural role models. For example, the president of the United States is, arguably, on any given day of the week, the most photographed person in the world. Even when leaders fail and are found to be fakers and fraudulent, we are fascinated by their skullduggery and duplicity; for example, Dennis Kozlowski of Tyco, Bernard Ebbers of WorldCom, Jeff Skilling and Ken Lay of Enron, and Bernard L. Madoff of Investment Securities.

But even if our collective social fascination with leaders and leadership is totally excessive, leadership plays a crucial role in the formulation of the business or ethics equation. We are convinced that without the continuous commitment, enforcement, and modeling of leadership, standards of business ethics cannot and will not be achieved in an organization. The ethics of leadership—whether it be good or bad, positive or negative—affects the ethos of the workplace and thereby helps to influence the ethical choices and decisions of both the workplace and the workers. Leaders help to set the tone, develop the vision, and shape the behavior of all those involved in organizational life. The critical point to understand here is that business and politics serve as the metronome of our society. The meter established by leaders sets the pattern and establishes the model for our individual and group behavior.

The fundamental principle that underlies our thesis regarding leadership, leaders, and ethical conduct is age old. In his *Nichomachean Ethics*, Aristotle suggested that morality cannot be learned by simply reading a treatise on virtue. The spirit of morality, said Aristotle, is awakened in the individual only through witnessing the conduct of a moral person. However, in claiming that workers or followers derive their models of ethical conduct from the behavior of leaders, we are not denying that workers or followers share responsibility for the overall conduct and culture of an organization. We are not trying to exonerate workers for their wrongdoing. We rather want to explain the process involved. Whether they are good or bad, moral or immoral, the conduct of leaders communicates the ethics of institutions. Although it would be naïve to assert that employees unreflectively absorb the manners and mores of the workplace, it would be equally naïve to suggest that they are unaffected by the modeling and standards of their respective places of employment. We spend our lives at work. The lessons we learn there, good or bad, play a significant part in the development of our moral perspective and the manner in which we formulate ethical choices.

According to ethicist Georges Enderle, business leadership would be relatively simple if businesses only had to produce a product or service, without being concerned about employees. Or, management only had to deal with concepts, structures, and strategies without worrying about human relations. Or, business just had to resolve their own problems, without being obligated to take the interest of other individuals into consideration.[2] But such is not the case. Leadership is always about self and others. Like ethics, business leadership is a symbiotic, communal relationship.

Like ethics, business leadership seems to be an intrinsic part of the human experience. Former French president and World War II hero Charles DeGaulle once observed that men can no more survive without direction than they can without eating, drinking, or sleeping. Leadership is a necessary requirement of communal existence. Minimally, it tries to offer perspective, focus, appropriate behavior, guidance, and a plan by which to handle the seemingly random and arbitrary events of life. Depending on the type of leadership involved, it can be achieved by consensus, fiat, or cooperative orchestration. But whatever techniques are used, leadership should always be about stewardship. A steward is "a person(s) who manages or directs the affairs of others . . . as an agent or representative of others."[3] It's about service over interest. To paraphrase the words of St. Augustine, regardless of the outcome, the first and final job of leadership is the attempt to serve the needs and the well-being of the people that they lead.

A DEFINITION

The terms *leader* and *leadership* are not synonyms. We really only understand leadership when we witness the conduct of a leader. Given this caveat, and leaning heavily on the research and insights of many others,[4] we can define leadership as follows: *Leadership is a power-and-value-laden relationship among leaders and followers/ constituents who share a common vision and intend real changes that reflect their mutual purpose and goals.* For our purposes, the critical elements of this definition that need to be examined are in order of importance: power, vision, values, followership, and mutual purposes and goals.

Power: The term *power* comes from the Latin *posse:* to do, to be able to change, to influence or effect. To have power is to possess the capacity to control or direct change. All forms of leadership must make use of power. Bertrand Russell called power the fundamental concept in social science, "in the same sense in which energy is a fundamental concept in physics."[5] However, power need not be coercive, dictatorial, or punitive to be effective. Power can also be used in a noncoercive manner to guide members of an organization in the pursuit of a goal or series of changes. The central issue of power in leadership is not "Will it be used?" but rather "Will it be used wisely and well?" In the best of all possible worlds, those who seek power would seek it out of a sense of stewardship and not for personal aggrandizement or career advancement.

Vision: Leaders need to create and communicate a clear vision of what they stand for, what they value, what they want to achieve, and what they expect from others. As former Herman Miller CEO Max De Pree succinctly put it: "The first responsibility of a leader is to define reality." The need to articulate a specific agenda and vision is critical to the leadership enterprise. In a very real sense, all forms of successful leadership are based on a shared vision that "binds those that lead with those who follow into some moral, intellectual, and emotional commitment."[6] However, even though vision is central to leadership, the visions offered need not always be Nobel Prize–winning accomplishments or involve Herculean efforts. For success to be possible, visions must be doable, attainable. Any task or vision—no matter how vital or important—when too large, will, more often than not, prove too overwhelming to accomplish or even attempt. At the very least, the visions of leadership must offer direction as well as hope.

Values: All of life is value-laden. As Samuel Blumenfeld empathically pointed out, "You have to be dead to be value-neutral."[7] Values are the ideas and beliefs that direct our choices and actions. Whether they are good or bad, values guide how we make decisions and influence the kinds of decisions we make.

All leadership, whether good or bad, is moral leadership at the descriptive, if not the normative, level. To put it more accurately, all leadership is motivated by a certain philosophical perspective, which upon analysis and judgment may or may not prove to be morally acceptable in the colloquial sense. All leaders have an agenda, a series of beliefs, proposals, values, ideas, and issues that they wish to "put on the table." In fact, as political theorist James MacGregor Burns suggested, leadership only asserts itself, and followers only become evident, when there is something at stake—ideas to be clarified, issues to be determined, values to be adjudicated.[8]

All of this raises the question: How do we judge the ethics of a leader? In *Character: America's Search for Leadership*, Gail Sheehy argues, as did Aristotle before her, that character is the most crucial and most elusive element of leadership. As we mentioned earlier, the root of the word *character* comes from the Greek word for *engraving*. As applied to human beings, it refers to the enduring marks or etched-in factors in our personality, which includes our inborn talents as well as the learned and acquired traits imposed on us by experience. These engravings define us, set us apart, and motivate behavior.

In regard to leadership, Sheehy says character is fundamental and prophetic. The "issues [of leadership] are today and will change in time. Character is what was yesterday and will be tomorrow."[9] Character establishes both our day-to-day demeanor and our destiny. Therefore, it is not only useful but also essential to examine the character of those who desire to lead us. As a journalist and longtime observer of the political scene, Sheehy contends that the Watergate affair of the early 1970s serves as a public example of the links between character and leadership. As Richard Nixon demonstrated so well, says Sheehy, "The Presidency is not the place to work out one's personal pathology."[10] Leaders rule us, run things, wield power. Therefore, says Sheehy, we must be careful about whom we choose to lead, because whom we chose is what we shall be. If, as Heraclitus wrote, "character is fate," the fate our leaders reap will also be our own.

The acid test of character is moral courage. Moral courage is a stimulus, a catalyst for action. Moral courage is the readiness to endure danger for the sake of principle.[11] Moral courage rejects voyeurism and seeks engagement. As Nelson Mandela has suggested, moral courage is not the absence of fear; rather, it is the strength to triumph over one's fear and to act.[12] Moral courage is the ability to transcend fear and endure risk. It is the ability to put ethics into actual practice. It means standing up and standing out in defense of a principle. Without it, ethics would simply be a naming noun and not an action word, a verb.

Followership: Perhaps the single most important thesis developed in leadership studies in the last twenty years has been the evolution and now almost universal consensus regarding the role of followers in the leadership equation. Pulitzer Prize–winning historian Garry Wills argues that we have long had a list of the leader's requisites—determination, focus, a clear goal, a sense of priorities, and so on. But until recently we overlooked or forgot the first and all-encompassing need. "The leader most needs followers. When those are lacking, the best ideas, the strongest will, the most wonderful smile have no effect."[13] Followers set the terms of acceptance for leadership. Leadership is a "mutually determinative" activity on the part of the leaders and the followers. Sometimes it's cooperative, sometimes it's a struggle, and often it's a feud, but it's always collective. Although "the leader is the one who mobilizes others towards a goal shared by leaders and followers," leaders are powerless to act without followers. In effect, Wills argues, successful leaders need to understand their followers far more than followers need to understand leaders.[14]

Leadership, like ethics, is always plural; it always occurs in the context of others. E. P. Hollander has argued that while the leader is the central and often the most vital part of the leadership phenomenon, followers are important and necessary factors in the equation.[15] All leadership is interactive, and all leadership should be collaborative. In fact, except for the negative connotation sometimes associated with the term, perhaps the word *collaborator* is a more precise term than either *follower* or *constituent* to explain the leadership process.[16] But whichever term is used, as James MacGregor Burns wrote, one thing is clear, "Leaders and followers are engaged in a common enterprise; they are dependent on each other, their fortunes rise and fall together."[17]

From an ethical perspective, the argument for the stewardship responsibilities of leadership is dependent upon the recognition of the roles and rights of followers. Followership argues against the claim of Louis XIV, "*L'état c'est moi!*" The principle of followership denies the Machiavellian assertations that "politics and ethics don't mix" and that the sole aim of any leader is "the acquisition of personal power." Followership requires that leaders recognize their true role within the commonwealth. The choices and actions of leaders must take into consideration the rights and needs of followers. Leaders are not independent agents simply pursuing personal aggrandizement and career options. Like the "Guardians" of Socrates' *Republic*, leaders must see their office as a social responsibility, a trust, a duty, and not a symbol of their personal identity, prestige, and lofty status.[18]

Mutual Purpose and Goals: The character, goals, and aspirations of a leader are not developed in a vacuum. Leadership, even in the hands of a strong, confident, charismatic leader remains, at bottom, relational. Leaders, good or bad, great or small, arise out of the needs and opportunities of a specific time and place. Leaders require causes, issues, and, most important, a hungry and willing constituency. Leaders may devise plans, establish an agenda, bring new and often radical ideas to the table, but all of them are a response to the milieu and membership of which they are a part. If leadership is an active and ongoing relationship between leaders and followers, then a central requirement of the leadership process is for leaders to evoke and elicit consensus in their constituencies, and conversely for followers to inform and influence their leaders.

According to James MacGregor Burns, leadership is not just about power-directed results. It is also about offering followers a choice among real alternatives. Hence, leadership assumes competition, conflict, and debate, whereas brute power denies it.[19] "Leadership mobilizes," says Burns, "naked power coerces."[20] Leaders must engage followers, not merely direct them. Leaders must serve as models and mentors, not martinets. According to Dwight D. Eisenhower, "You don't lead by hitting people over the head—that's assault, not leadership."[21]

CONCLUSION

Leadership is a serious, but not necessarily a sacred, duty or task. Peter Drucker argues that leadership, by itself, is not a good or desirable thing. It is rather a means to an end. For Drucker, the main purpose and the justification for all forms of leadership is to make human efforts more productive and to enable common individuals to do uncommon things. *Businessweek*, in agreement with Drucker's thesis, has pointed out that there is a direct correlation between corporate profits, well-run companies, and strong, effective leadership. Their studies show that having the right man or woman in the corner suite may, in fact, be more important in bad times than in good. But, they argue, it is of course best to have the right person there all the time.[22]

Leadership is hard to exactly define, and moral leadership is even harder. Perhaps, like Justice Stewart with pornography, we only recognize moral leadership when we see it. The problem is, we so rarely see it. Nevertheless, we are convinced that without the "witness" of moral leadership, standards of ethics in business and organizational life will not readily emerge and be sustained. Leadership, even when defined as a collaborative experience, is still about the influence of individual character and the impact of personal mentoring. Leaders can be the catalyst for morally sound behavior, but they are not by themselves a sufficient condition. By means of their demeanor and message, leaders must be able to convince, not just tell others, that collaboration serves the conjoint interest and well-being of all involved. Leaders may offer a vision, but followers must buy into it. Leaders must organize a plan, but followers must decide to take it on. Behavior does not always beget like behavior in a one-to-one ratio, but it does establish tone, set the stage, and offer options. Although to achieve ethical behavior an organization, from top to bottom, must make a commitment to it, and the model for that commitment has to originate from the top.[23] And, to return to the central theme of this text, in the end, leadership, like ethics, "is first and last an exercise in reason—the ideas that should come out on top are the ones that have the best reasons on their side."[24]

NOTES

1. Portions of this chapter are drawn from Al Gini, "Moral Leadership and Business Ethics," Working Papers of the Kellogg Leadership Studies Project (College Park, Md.: University of Maryland, 1996).

2. Georges Enderle, "Some Perspectives on Managerial Ethical Leadership," *Journal of Business Ethics* 6 (1987): 657.

3. P. Block, *Stewardship: Choosing Security over Self-Interest* (San Francisco, Calif.: Jossey-Bass, 1996), pp. xx, 6.

4. Joseph C. Rost, *Leadership for the Twenty-First Century* (Westport, Conn.: Praeger, 1993).

5. James MacGregor Burns, *Leadership* (New York: Harper Torchbooks, 1979), p. 12.

6. Abraham Zaleznick, "The Leadership Gap," *Academy of Management Executives* 4 (1) (1990): 12.

7. Christina Hoff Sommers, "Teaching the Virtues," *Chicago Tribune Magazine* (September 12, 1993): 16.

8. Burns, chapters 2, 5.

9. Gail Sheehy, *Character: America's Search for Leadership* (New York: Bantam Books, 1990), p. 311.

10. Ibid., p. 66.

11. Rushworth Kidder, *Moral Courage* (New York: Harper Collins, 2005), p. 7.

12. Richard Stengel, "Mandela: His 8 Lessons of Leadership," *Time* (July 9, 2008).

13. Garry Wills, *Certain Trumpets* (New York: Simon and Schuster, 1994), p. 13.

14. Ibid., 17.

15. E. P. Hollander, *Leadership Dynamics* (New York: The Free Press, 1978), pp. 4, 5, 6, 12.

16. See Joseph Rost, "Leadership Development in the New Millennium," *Journal of Leadership Studies* 1 (1993): 109, 110.

17. Burns, p. 426.

18. Al Gini, "Moral Leadership: An Overview," *Journal of Business Ethics* 16 (1997): 323–330.

19. Burns, p. 66.

20. Ibid., p. 439.

21. Patrick M. Morgan, *Re-Viewing the Cold War: Domestic Factors and Foreign Policy in the East-West Confrontation* (Westport, Conn.: Praeger, 2000), p. 47.

22. *BusinessWeek*, "The CEO Conundrum" (June 15, 2009): 12.

23. Maynard M. Dolecheck and Carolyn C. Dolecheck, "Ethics: Take It from the Top," *Business* (JanuaryMarch 1989): 13, 14.

24. James Rachels, *The Elements of Moral Philosophy* (New York: Random House, 1986), p. vi.

INDEX

ABOUT THE AUTHORS

Al Gini is professor of business ethics and chair of the Department of Management in the School of Business Administration at Loyola University Chicago. He is also the cofounder and longtime associate editor of *Business Ethics Quarterly*, the journal of the Society for Business Ethics. He lectures regularly to community and professional organizations on issues in business ethics, and for over twenty-three years has been the resident philosopher on Chicago's National Public Radio affiliate, WBEZ-FM. His books include *My Job My Self: Work and the Creation of the Modern Individual* (2000); *The Importance of Being Lazy: In Praise of Play, Leisure and Vacations* (2003); *Why It's Hard to Be Good* (2006); *Seeking The Truth of Things* (2010); and *God Can Quote Me On That* (2011).

Alexei Marcoux is associate professor of business ethics in the School of Business Administration at Loyola University Chicago. Writing widely on the topic of business ethics, his articles appear in academic and public policy journals such as *Business Ethics Quarterly*, *Cato Policy Report*, *Journal of Business Ethics*, *Journal of Markets & Morality*, and *Journal of Private Enterprise*. He is also a contributor to the edited volumes *Normative Theory and Business Ethics* (2008) and *Corporate Governance and Business Ethics* (2011). He thanks the

Social Philosophy & Policy Center at Bowling Green State University and its directors Fred Miller, Ellen Paul, and Jeff Paul for a visiting scholarship in 2004 during which central ideas for this book were outlined. He also thanks Liberty Fund, Inc. and its leadership team of Chris Talley, Emilio Pacheco, and Doug Den Uyl for a resident scholarship in 2008 during which portions of this book were drafted.